Other books by Dave Galey

The Bus Converter's Bible

The Joys of Busing

The Motor Coaching Bible

Slide Out Rooms, Mechanics and Structures

Classy Cabinets for Converted Coaches

Fascinating Fastener Facts

Black & Blue Highways

Eagle Planning Sheets

The Gospel of Gauges

Busin' Bits

Bus Wiring for Bus Nuts
an
Electrifying Process

with simple
Step-by-Step
Instructions

Dave Galey

Bus Wiring for Bus Nuts
an
Electrifying Process
using simple
Step-by-Step
Instructions

Published by:
  WINLOCK Publishing Co.
  26135 Murrieta Road
  Sun City, California 92585

ISBN: 1-890461-07-5

Price: $29.95

Warning - Disclaimer

This book is designed to provide information only on the subject matter covered. It is sold with the understanding that the publisher and author are not engaged in rendering legal, accounting, engineering, or other professional services. If legal or other expert assistance is required, the services of a competent professional should be sought.

It is not the purpose of this manual to reprint all the information otherwise available to the author and/or publisher, but to complement, amplify and supplement other texts. You are urged to read all the available material, learn as much as possible about bus conversion and to tailor the information to your individual needs.

Every effort has been made to make this manual as complete and as accurate as possible. However, there may be mistakes both typographical and in content. Therefore, this text should be used only as a general guide and not as the ultimate source of electrical panel and fabrication for bus conversions. Furthermore, this manual contains information on bus conversion only up to the printing date.

The purpose of this manual is to educate and entertain. The author and **WINLOCK GALEY** shall have neither liability nor responsibility to any person or entity with respect to any loss or damage caused, or alleged to be caused, directly or indirectly by the information contained in this book.

If you do not wish to be bound by the above, you may return this book to the publisher for a full refund.

Dedicated to Dick Wright
alway ready to help

Contents

Introduction

The purpose of this book is to guide one through the wiring process using a step-by-step method. We list a minimum number of tools required and illustrate some of the parts needed.

First we must understand a little about the nature of electricity. We build on the concept of the extension cord to describe a circuit. Ideas are presented for wire routing. Power sources are described and a block diagram is built up in a logical sequence to illustrate all the requirements of the modern bus conversion.

Suggestions are presented for circuits, circuit breakers and wiring diagrams. Enough theory is given so a reader may custom design his own system. A number of tables are shown depicting the power demand of various appliances. Reference tables are presented listing the amperage capacity of wire sizes.

DAVE GALEY

Electricity

Electricity is without a doubt, one of the most mysterious entities in existence. It has the capacity to generate freezing and also heat. It can also move heavy objects and light up our lives. I do not profess to know what electricity is, but I can envision some parallels to water.

To begin with, imagine a full water tank up on 10 foot stilts. If you tapped into the tank at water level with a pipe, the pressure would be zero. If it was a 10 foot deep tank and you tapped into it at the bottom, the pressure would be 10 feet of water, or approximately 4 pounds per square inch. This number is derived from the fact that a one square inch column of water a foot high weighs about four-tenths of a pound, or almost 7 ounces. Actually, the precise number is 0.433527777 pounds per square inch at sea level on a standard day. But, the data given above is close enough for our discussion. If you measured the pressure in your hose at ground level it would be over 8 psi (pounds per square inch). If you dug a ten foot hole and dropped your hose to the bottom, the water pressure would be over 13 psi at the outlet.

Why, do you ask, if this is about electricity, what is all the hydraulics about? OK, here's the answer. All this talk about water and it's pressure is to enlighten the reader that much of electricity can be related to hydraulics. In electricity, voltage is akin to water pressure. For example: 120 volts is tens times the pressure of 12 volts, and only half the pressure of 240 volts.

As the in the water analogy, if you have a small pipe with a lot of pressure, you may be able to transport the same volume as with a larger pipe and less pressure. In the same manner, if you have large wires, with a low voltage, you may be able to deliver the same amperage as with a high voltage and a smaller wire. So, we can equate volume (or quantity) of water to amperes, or current.

Finally, energy is measured in watts, which is a specific amount of energy over a specific time period. For convenience we use the hour as the time measure of energy. So, as in the water analogy, pressure times amount of water equals a volume, in the same manner, voltage times amperage equals a specific volume of electrical work.

At this point, it is important to equate this volume of electrical work to the time element. That is, if an electrical device uses 1200 watts, such as a microwave oven, but is only on for 6 minutes, it will consume 10 amps of current, but for only one-tenth of an hour. So in effect, this appliance uses one ampere of energy, or 120 watts of power. Understand, however, if the appliance is supported by an inverter drawing on a 12 volt battery bank, the power drawn from the batteries is ten times higher since we have one-tenth the voltage, i.e., 12 volts. Therefore, the batteries will deliver 10 amp-hours, to run the microwave oven for six minutes. Actually, there exists a friction loss, plus an over head due to heating and other losses in the inverter, so the battery bank may lose some what more than 10 A/H (amp-hours.)

Now, lets discus the types of electricity; direct current and alternating current. Direct current is very simple to under stand since it has a positive and negative. A battery produces direct current. It is akin to the water tank analogy. The pressure pushes the amperes from the high level to the low level. That is from the positive side to the negative side. Another interesting thing is that you may have a switch on either side of a device to control it. That is, you may have the battery positive terminal wired to an on/off switch and then to the device and from the device to ground or the negative side of the battery. On the other hand, you may wire from the positive terminal of the battery to the device and then to an on/off switch and finally to the negative terminal, or ground. A simple switch can be equated to a valve in the water analogy. A water turbine is controlled by a faucet which may be at either side of the turbine, i.e., upstream or downstream

One of the neat things about direct current is you can find a ground or negative location almost anywhere on the coach. Once the negative terminal of the battery is connect to the bus framework, any metallic location contiguous with the frame will return the direct current to ground.

Alternating current is similar to direct current except that it pulses in one direction and then another. These pressure pulses in the U.S. normally occur 60 times each second. In Europe, a 50 cycle current is common.

Circuits

What are electrical circuits. Well, obviously, the noun circuit means a path. So, a circuit is a path. The simplest path is a trip to and from a specific point. If we consider a lamp cord from a wall socket to a lamp as a simple path to and from a specific point, then we can deem this to be a circuit.

Now, lets add another appliance to the wall socket. This is the same thing as adding another circuit. So, an electrical circuit can be as simple as a to and from path. OK, lets say this lamp also has a built-in socket so we can add another item to the lamp. We now have a continuation of the circuit from the wall socket. This is equivalent to a parallel circuit. That is electricity is delivered to both the lamp and the lamp socket in an equal voltage, or pressure level.

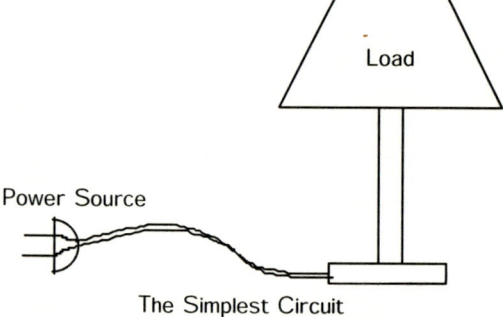

The Simplest Circuit

To depict this lamp circuit in a conventional electrical diagram, we have:

A circuit may be as simple as a to and from pathway, or it may be as complex as one wishes. For example, the simple lamp circuit shown on the previous page may have a switch added. It may also have a circuit protector added, such as a breaker. It could continue as a buss bar with the lamp, switch and breaker as a branch. Then it could have several branches leading from it to other appliances. Or, it could have the fuse, or breaker up front at the beginning and have only switches to individual appliances.

A typical circuit in a residential application would have a circuit breaker, or fuse, providing power to a half dozen wall sockets, (convenience outlets.) Once a fuse experiences too much current, it burns through and must be replaced. Fuses are almost extinct expect for specific applications such as protecting air conditioner units. Today almost all circuits are protected with re-settable circuit breakers.

Why do we need fuses, or circuit breakers? A very high current becomes very hot and can ignite a fire. For example an arc welder is simply a device for delivering a current high enough to melt metal. Now, lets consider our lamp circuit. Our dog runs though the place and knocks over the lamp. The lamp shatters, stripping some wire insulation and causes power wires to touch each other. Since there is no load between the wires, they will demand unlimited current to flow producing a temperature limited only by the melt temperature of the conductors. This is called a short circuit, or simply a *short*. This high temperature may then cause a fire.

Incidentally, we commonly, and mistakenly call a convenience outlet a *wall plug*. A plug is a male object whereas a receptacle is a female object. So much for sex!

We have now come to understand the concept of a circuit. Each circuit could have it's origin at different and random locations, but that would not be very practical. So, since our power source is delivered to our unit at a single location, it is practical to use this location, or one nearby, to distribute our power throughout our unit. (Notice how I cleverly refer to our **unit**, which may be our home, our boat, or our bus.)

At this point it is practical to gather all our circuit breakers to a single location and panel mount them. Hence we have the term *distribution panel*. The place from which all power is distributed throughout the coach.

So, it is convenient to consider each circuit nothing more than an extension cord plugged into the distribution panel, where the breakers are located.

Power Distribution

Now that we understand a circuit is nothing more than an extension cord, we can plan how to arrange these various extension cords, which will be our power distribution.

High current draw items such as air conditioners, water heaters and space heaters often are supplied by their own circuit. A 1200 watt microwave, for example, may have a dedicated circuit with it's own breaker.

The tables on the following pages shown a suggested process for breaking down our power requirements into separate circuits. For example: convenience outlets, commonly rated at 15 amps, may be divided into a circuit on the left side and one on the right side of the bus and protected with a 20 amp breaker. Lets say you have six outlets on each side of the bus. Oops!, that adds up to six times a 15 amp outlet which is equal to 90 amps. However, the chances of all six outlets being in use simultaneously and each demanding 15 amps is so remote as to be dismissed. Lets assume this circuit has a toaster in use at 10 amps and two lamps at one amp each. This only adds up to 12 amps. It would be possible to trip the circuit breaker if your wife was running a hair dryer at 10 amps and a toaster is on at 12 amps along with a couple of lights. A simple solution to this possibility would be to remove the bathroom circuit, where a hair dryer might be used, from the string of convenience outlets.

Now for a quick lesson in the laws of nature and power.

Amperage draw = Power in wattage divided by the voltage pressure.

Appliances are rated in wattage and voltage. If the voltage drops below the rating, the appliance will draw more current to keep operating. And, since it is stupid, it doesn't understand that by drawing more current, it may burn itself out, and it does just that.

One other point to keep in mind, alternating current voltage can vary from 108 volts to 130 volts and still be within tolerance. therefore, a 1200 watt appliance may draw as much as 11.12 amps, or a little as 9.25 amps. So, it is important when determining your circuitry, this tolerance be considered..

The following tables list some common electrical appliances along with their wattage and current draw.

Appliances	Avg. Required Wattage	Est. Amps
Sewing Machine	125	1.0
Space Heater	1000-1500	8-13
Television	200-600	1.5-4
Toaster	750-1200	6.5-10
Washer/Dryer	2000-2250	16
VCR	150-200	1.15

Appliances	Avg. Required Wattage	Est. Amps
Air Conditioner	1400-2200	12-18
Battery Charger	Up to 800	6-7
Blender	600	5.5
Broiler	1350	12
Coffee pot	550-700	4-6
Compact Disc Player & Speaker	50-100	0.5-0.9
Computer	50-200	0.5-1.8
Converter	300-350	2-3
Hair Dryer	1200	10
Dishwasher	1400	12
Blanket	50-200	0.5-1.5
Broom/Vacuum	200-500	1.5-4

Appliances	Avg. Required Wattage	Est. Amps
Drill	250-750	2-6
Fan	25-100	0.2-0.9
Frying Pan/Wok	1000-1350	8-11
Stove (per element)	350-1000	3-8
Winter Heater	1000-1500	8-13
Water Pump	500-600	4-5
Hair Dryer	350-1000	3-8
Iron	500-1200	4-10
Light Bulbs	40-100 each	0.36-0.9
Microwave	700-1500	6-13
Radio	50-200	0.5-1.5
Refrigerator	600-1000	5-8

Sample Circuit Distribution

The drawing on the next page depicts a proposed bus layout with an extension slide, (which is optional) and it's electrical distribution. The circuits are:

Circuit no.	Appliances	Breaker Size
1	Forward Air Conditioner	30 amp
2	Rear Air conditioner	30 amp
3	LH Convenience outlets	20 amp
4	RH Convenience outlets	20 amp
5	Refrigerator	20 amp
6	Water heater	20 amp
7	Kitchen outlets	20 amp
8	Washer/Dryer	30 amp
9	Inverter Circuitry*	30 amp
10	Spare	Blank

* the inverter circuitry brings up a special concept we should now consider: **A sub panel.** This sub panel may be part of the mail panel in appearance, but be wired in a unique manner. What we do is to isolate any circuit which we do not want to be fed by the battery bank, by way of the inverter. For example, we do not want to run our air conditioners with batter power. Nor, do we want hot water created by battery power. And, most importantly, we definitely do not want to recharge our batteries with battery power.

The solution to this approach is to create a main panel which is fed by either shore power or generator power, and a sub panel which is fed by the main panel and the battery bank through the inverter. It is very feasible to allow the inverter to send power to the convenience outlets and normal kitchen appliances, such as a coffee maker and a microwave oven. In addition, any bathroom appliance may be supplied by the sub panel. The main criteria being, low power drain for a long period, such as a television, or computer, or a high power usage for a brief period such as a toaster, microwave oven, or a hair dryer.

Obviously, such appliances as air conditioners and water heaters that use high power for a long period would deplete the battery bank if supplied by the inverter.

The plan on the next page show a bus floor plan with a slide room. On the following pages are blank plans which may be used for concepting an electrical scheme.

12 Volt Circuits

Much of the lighting may be 12 volt. Or, one may mix and match, 12 volt lighting with 120 volt lighting. With the advent of the high efficiency inverter, with very little overhead loss, a 120 volt lamp may be used at nearly the same power drain as a 12 volt lamp. Furthermore, a greater variety of 120 volt lamps are available. One new 12 volt lamp is a halogen surface mounted lamp available from Lowes, or Home Depot. This small lamp is only about 2-1/2 inches in diameter.

Some of the essential 12 volt appliances in your bus will be:

1	Water pump(s)
2	Water heater igniter (if propane is used)
3	refrigerator (if RV frig is installed)
4	Baggage compartment lights
5	Ceiling vent fans
6	CBs & Automotive radios
7	Back up camera and monitor
8	12 lighting
9	Monitors for water tanks, etc.
10	Generator controls
11	Toilet (if electric)

Again, the plan is to separate your 12 volts appliances into circuits according to their usage and power drain. It is seldom necessary to exceed 20 amps for any 12 volt breaker. In fact, the Eagle bus automotive wiring uses 15 amps breakers exclusively.

Referring to the illustration on page 73, you will notice that there is a space on the drawing labelled electrical panel. It is important we dedicate an area on our floor pan to terminate all our wiring, where we will install our distribution panel.

This may be in the baggage compartment, but it would be more convenient in the main living section. It may be a space as small as 8 inches wide, or it may even be located over the refrigerator. Preferably, it would be set at eye level so we may examine the gauges and monitors with ease.

Not only would this panel include both the 120 volt and the 12 volt circuit breakers, but additional control and monitors should be installed. For example, this is a logical location for the generator start/stop control and gauges. In addition, we should install out inverter remote control in this panel. Finally, a master switch should be added along with all monitors for liquid levels.

It should be noted at this point, that although residential electrical panels may be used, they are often too big and do not contain enough breaker positions. It is much more professional to fabricate a custom panel designed specifically for your coach.

Therefore, the material in this book will show only custom designed and fabricate panels. The drawing on the next page shows a suggested panel design. The upper gauges are the generator monitor gauges along with the start/stop switch for the genset. Below that are a DC Voltage meter and an AC Voltage meter. Going down, we have a remote control panel for the inverter and finally, we have the breakers for the AC and the DC.

Wire Routing

I am often asked, "Where and how do you route your wiring and plumbing?" The answer to that question contains many options. In building construction, these conduits of the building's circulatory and nervous system are buried inside the walls, floors and ceilings. So, the obvious answer is to do the same thing. Right? Yes, but how?

We are fabricating a tiny house within a confined envelope and, as such, space is a valuable commodity. We would like to preserve all the inside width we can. However, where the floor meets the side-walls is normally a dead area. For example, you would seldom walk there or even sit there. There are exceptions though. If you have an island bed, then you will walk there. Another useful area is the space above the windows. Here we have an area normally shielded by a valance, or enclosed by an overhead cabinet.

One way to preserve interior width is to route the wiring through the structure. In the early days of electrification of residential construction, a technique known as *knob and tube* was used. This was where a ceramic tube was used to lead the wire through structure such as the studs and the terminal point, or radical changes in directions were accomplished by clamping the wires to ceramic knobs. In those days, wire insulation was a wax coated cotton braid.

A technique I have used recently is shown in the illustration. I wished to use a similar technique as today's residential construction whereby three-conductor cable, such as boat cable, was routed through the structure. Once process would have been to drill holes into the structural tubing and line each hole with a rubber or plastic grommet. It has been my experience that grommets sometime fail to stay where they are put, so I selected lengths of aluminum tubing to act as fairleads, or bushings, through the drilled holes. After the rough wiring is done, I had urethane foam sprayed in place, which stabilized all wires and cables. This is sort of like the encapsulation techniques of many electrical circuits. It does not, however, lend itself to future modifications.

I used 2 x 2 x 4 junction boxes, screw attached to the framework protruding 3/8ths of an inch so the J-box was flush with the 3/8 rough plywood of the interior. This technique maximizes the inside width of the coach.

Another method of wire routing would be to create a wire chase, 2 x 4 inches nestled along each wall to floor junction. This could be designed so the top of the chase is in removable sections. This way, modification could be done by simply removing a section of the top.

I have also seen PVC piping used as wiring conduits whereby large pipe, such as 1-½ inch diameter might be attached to the interior just above the side windows and used as a chase to route a number of circuits. Sections would be sliced out the pipe lengthwise where a circuit is needed for a specific location. Cabinets and valances would conceal the pipe conduit.

Some builders will create a utility chase along each side of the coach, of depending on the floor plan. Perhaps one chase would suffice if the kitchen and bath utilities were along the same wall. The utility chase would house, not only the wiring, but also the plumbing runs and the heating ducts plus any speaker, or television wiring. When the chase reached the bedroom area, it would turn upward and extend over the window headers in order to allow as much walking space as possible around an island bed.

As a policy, I recommend a number of spare wires be laid inside the coach tunnel terminating at locations convenient to the cockpit at one end and the engine electrical at the other. This bundle should be made up of not only various wire sizes but coaxial TV cable and quarter-inch nylon air tubing. This package may die with your coach unused, but in this day of miraculous developments, who knows what wonders lurk in the future?

Of course, the most obvious location for routing wiring is through the central floor tunnel. The main problem with this is servicing the side walls. The drawings below depict a couple of wire routing schemes. The bottom drawing show the utility chase usable for not only wiring but heating and plumbing.

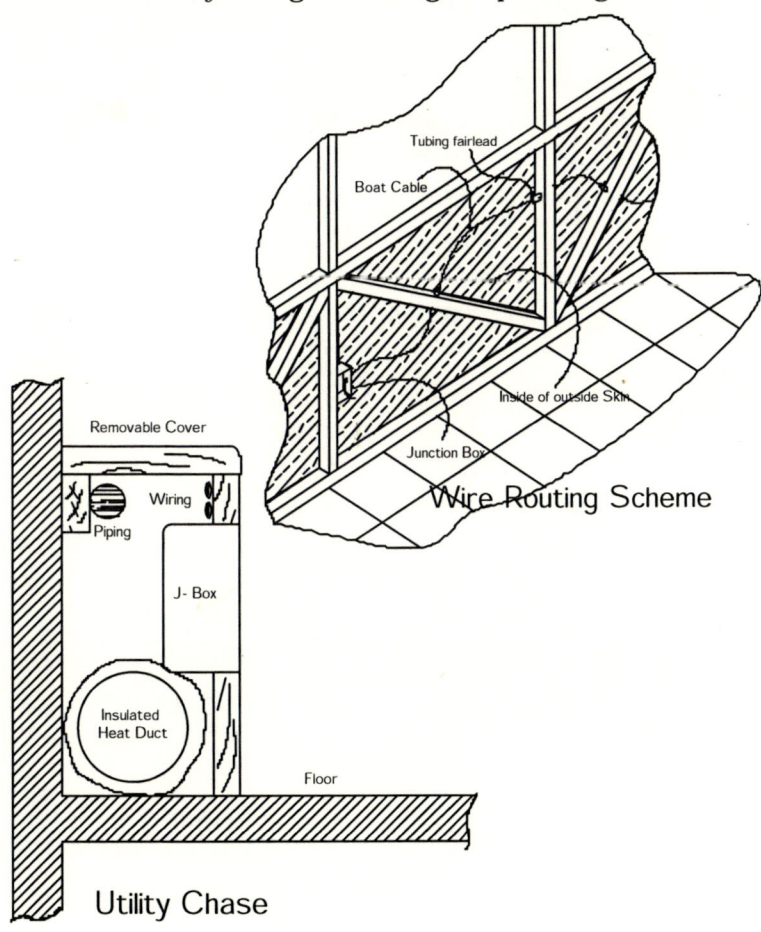

Tubing fairlead

Boat Cable

Inside of outside Skin

Removable Cover

Wiring

Piping

Junction Box

Wire Routing Scheme

J- Box

Insulated
Heat Duct

Floor

Utility Chase

Generators

Believe it or not, the average 200 amp residential service is provided by a 10,000 watt (10 KW) transformer. Now, I know that doesn't compute. 200 amps at 120 volts is 24 kilowatts. The reason I know this is true, is a tornado ripped out about a mile and a half of power lines along the street in front of our house. When the power company re-erected the power poles, they hung only a 10 KW transformer to convert the 24000 volts to 240 volt for my house. Being a smart-alecky engineer, I challenged them, declaring we had 200 amp service and we needed a 24 KW transformer. I was informed, that if the 10 KW did not do the job they would install a bigger one. Well, it's been ten years and we have not had a problem. These transformers are oil cooled and capable of large surge loads for a long period of time.

The size of the generator should be large enough to satisfy the demands of every appliance in the coach including their start-up load factor. Start-up load factors are not relevant in heating type devices such as lamps, heaters and televisions. Start-up factors should be considered with any type of rotating machinery, such as motors and air conditioners. Although these factors vary with the type of motor and the load conditions, it is important to use a load factor ranging from 5 to 7 on these applications. Even the modern rotary air conditioners with a running load of 15 amps need about 80 amps to start.

Generators may be set to provide either 240-volt alternating current (AC), or 120-volt AC. This is a preference to be made by the owner. By selecting the 240VAC option, two 120-volt legs may be run to the distribution panel, but the problem of balancing the loads must be solved. The advantages of the 240-volt option is one leg may be dedicated to relatively small loads for convenience, such as lighting and entertainment. This leg may then also be supplied by an inverter powered by the battery bank to provide electrical conveniences while the generator is not running. In balancing the load with a 240-volt system, it is obvious if two air conditioning units are used, each one should be supplied by each leg. One drawback with the inverter dedicated to one leg and an air conditioner also running on that leg is, if the generator were to shut down, the inverter would try to run the Air Conditioner (A/C) depleting the batteries and damaging the A/C. Other high load appliances should be as evenly shared by the two legs as possible. Another advantage to the 240-volt system, is the capability of operating high voltage equipment, such as an electric cook-top, or a welder directly from the generator. 120 VAC cooktops and welders, however, are available. As far as hooking up to shore power where only low voltage is available, the land line, or umbilical simply plugs into an adapter feeding both legs with a single hot lead. These adapters are available in RV supply stores. However, it must be cautioned, with this system 240-volt appliances could not be operated. In order to design for 240-volt appliances, a hot lead is employed from each leg, and the shore line must be plugged into a 240-volt source, a convenience not available in every trailer park.

Without a doubt, the simplest way to set up the generator is 120-volt AC. With this approach, there is no need to balance the load distribution. The inverter(s) may then serve a selected group of appliances through a sub-panel. The battery bank delivering power to the inverter, however, must be capable of supplying all the electrical demands of this sub panel. If the battery bank is too small to achieve these demands, it is mandatory the inverter be able to be switched out of the system in the event the generator is providing power, but fails for some reason. If this were to happen, the battery bank would be depleted in short order.

Generators are available in gasoline, propane, or diesel

power. Since our conversions are primarily powered with diesel fuel, it is logical to select a diesel powered generator. Many conversions do use both diesel and propane. Although propane does not have the efficiency that diesel fuel has, it is an extremely clean burning fuel. In addition, propane fueled motors remain exceptionally clean.

If a diesel fueled generator is selected because it is the common fuel of the primary coach engine, it is important not to simply "tee-off" from the coach fuel line. The coach engine pump moves well over sixty gallons of fuel per hour. This would probably starve the generator if an attempt were made to run them simultaneously. So, it is imperative a separate fuel line and return fuel line be dedicated to the generator.

The generator should be mounted in a clean compartment with a flow of fresh air available. This fresh air may be achieved by installing a blower or fan. The radiator for the generator may be remotely mounted, as long as it too has a supply of clean, fresh, cool air. For example, it would not be wise to mount the generator radiator in the coach engine compartment where it would be subject to the hot air radiating from the motor. A logical location would be a baggage compartment behind the forward axle bulkhead, where a source of cooling air may be obtained between the steering tires. Another common acceptable practice is to connect the generator cooling system into the coach cooling system. This has the advantage that the coach engine temperature gauges will also reflect the generator engine temperature.

It is recommended the generator be mounted in a frame or cage which may be rolled out or swung out in order to simplify maintenance, although some generators may be serviced from only one side. It is recommended the exhaust from the generator be directed to a remote location while parked next to other coaches. An ideal solution would be to direct the exhaust through the roof of the coach. This may be done by routing the exhaust pipe through a slightly larger section of transite, cement pipe, or other form of insulating conduit.

A small editorial note might be appropriate at this point. Commonly we hear house voltage referred to as 110 volts, or 115 volts, or even 117 volts. And, we often hear the higher voltage referred to as 220. Voltage is derived as a result of the division of the transmission of very high voltage. Although the value of the transmitted voltage varies according to the distance and the terrain, one of the more common transmission voltages is 12,000 volts. Step down transformers are then employed to divide this transmitted voltage down to 480 volts, and 240 volts. Almost all voltage delivered to a residence through a step down transformer is 240 volts. Appliance makers often refer to a design operating voltage of 117. This is to compensate for voltage drops as a result of normal line loss due to conductor resistance. At anytime, a meter may be applied to a wall outlet in a house and the voltage will fluctuate from about 108 on the low side to as high as 124. These fluctuations are caused by a myriad of reasons, from public demand to sun spots. As is obvious from the discussion above, I prefer to stick to the simplicity of multiples of 120. The principle advantage this has, it is easily divisible by the most common direct current voltage, i.e.., 12 and 24 volts.

One very important accessory for the generator should be considered. This is an automatic start device that may be added for about ten percent additional cost to the generator. This automatic start system may be triggered by several options. One option built into the system, is a low battery condition. This will sense a low battery bank, turn on your generator, recharge your batteries to a specific level, then shut itself off. The low battery sensor is designed to sample your voltage over a time period so it will not start the generator simply because of a transitory condition. Another form of sensor, samples the outside temperature. This sensor may be set for a low temperature so your generator may turn on and drive electric heaters to warm your coach, or to sense a high temperature so that your air conditioning may be powered on automatically. Obviously, manual controls are built in so you may turn off this feature if you don't want it operable while you are sleeping. This accessory has a built in alarm buzzer warning anyone in near proximity it is about to start. Finally, the number of start attempts may be adjusted, since sometimes motors do not always start on the first try. This can be set for maximum reliability.

Converters, Inverters, and Chargers

A converter is basically a device which converts alternating current, like standard residential current to direct current through a *rectifier*. A *rectifier* is basically a large step down transformer with diodes, or electrical check valves which force the alternating current to emerge as a directional one way current. This permits the converter to act like a battery charger. In addition, a converter will have a series of fuse holders so a direct current system of circuits may be distributed throughout the coach. Converters are not as often seen with the advance of solid state devices.

An inverter is an electrical device which does the opposite of a converter. It takes direct current and changes it to alternating current, such as we have in our houses. The earlier inverters were direct current motors driving an alternator. The most common unit was made by Honeywell, known as a Readyline. Readyline, and Powerline are trademarks of Honeywell. These units were available in 500, 1000 and 1500 watts. No doubt, larger sizes were available, but not as common. The principle problem with the motor driven inverters was the high overhead in battery power needed to operate them. For example, a 1000-watt unit could run a television which used only 120 watts. But instead of drawing 10 amps from the battery bank, it would draw over 15 amps. This was because a minimum power drain was used to simply turn the rotor. This results in a poor efficiency rating for the rotating style of the inverter; on the order of 55 to 70 percent. Additionally, the rotating inverter has a whine which can get on your nerves if you are sensitive to noise. These are quite a few drawbacks, but in the earlier days, it was the only game in town.

The solid state inverter has been around for a number of years, but the earlier ones also had a relatively poor efficiency rating. Tripp is a brand name which comes to mind. The earlier solid state inverters also had an annoying hum, or buzz. In recent years, we have seen the development of the computerized solid state inverters with no moving parts. These units are made by Trace, Best, Heart and no doubt, others. These companies have most aggressively entered the RV market. The units are commonly available in 2,000, 2,500, and 5,000 watts. For greater power requirements they may be stacked, or cascaded. This means they may be installed so that their power capabilities are added together to provide all the power a coach needs. In addition, a common inverter option is a built-in battery charger. With the addition of a simple fuse holder for direct current applications, the need for a converter disappears. Another option instead of a fuse holder, is a bank of re-settable circuit breakers for direct current applications. Inverters have other options such as remote readout panels, and remote on/off controls. The readout panels will display such information as the battery voltage, charging rate in amps, the peak to peak input voltage, and the frequency of the alternating current. The frequency readout feature is especially useful when setting the speed of the generator drive engine, in the event you receive your generator in an un-calibrated condition or in case the generator motor has to be repaired.

Battery chargers are an essential piece of equipment. They are simply a source of direct current connected in parallel with the battery system. A battery charger is generally set to provide a direct current at 13.8 volts. This value permits the batteries to recharge, but not boil out the battery acid. In many respects storage batteries may be equated to pails of power, similar to buckets of water. If two batteries were placed side by side with different charges and were connected, the higher charge would pour over into the lesser charge. After a time their charges would be equal. This is similar to *water seeking its own level*. In a simplified manner, this is basically what a battery charger does. A bank of batteries whose reading may be 12.3 volts, when connected to a 13.8 volt charging system will, ultimately, come up to 13.8 volts over a period of time. The charger will begin by charging at a high rate, but will, as the voltage builds up in the batteries, taper down to a trickle, hence the term *trickle charge.*

A very sophisticated form of charger is now available for a fairly high cost. This is a marine pulse charger. A unit rated at only 20 amps can cost over $400. A pulse charger is a unique concept in that it has been determined a storage battery would prefer to accept replenishing charges in small doses, instead of a continuous flow. These pulse chargers have been known to restore a depleted battery which has been judged ready for the scrap heap.

Another interesting form of battery charger is the photovoltaic cell or group of cells known as solar panels. This is the passive charging system . Many of us are familiar with the LED (light emitting diode), a small device that lights up when a voltage is impressed across it. The photovoltaic cell is the opposite of the LED. If a light is shone on the photovoltaic cell, it will yield a voltage. A large array of these cells are combined together to form a solar panel. Solar panels are available in many voltages and power combinations. In the very early days of the solar panel, they were selling for about three dollars per watt; very expensive even by today's standard. It was predicted then the price of the solar panel would ultimately descend to about thirty cents a watt. Because of manufacturing difficulties and a monopoly this never happened and the price of solar panels is still quite high. For approximately 400 plus dollars, however, solar panels may be mounted on the roof of a conversion to provide a battery charging capability from the sun, or even a street lamp. Since many of the solar panels are designed to put out about 18 volts, a voltage regulator is necessary. The voltage of a solar panel is not a constant thing because of the varying intensity of the impinging light. Obviously, on a bright sunny day with the sun nearly overhead, more voltage will be generated than on a dull overcast day with the late afternoon sun.

Wind generators have been available for many years, but I know of no practical unit available for the RV industry. I recall a small wind driven generator to light a lamp on my bicycle which I had as a kid.

Finally, the most common form of battery charger is the motor driven alternator mounted on the primary engine. The more modern units have built-in regulator/rectifying diodes so a voltage regulator is becoming a thing of the past. These are used primarily to maintain the starting batteries, and provide power for the lighting, and automotive accessories. However, a simple circuit will be described in a later chapter so the alternator charges the house batteries as you travel down the road.

Battery Requirements

Batteries are rated in amp-hours. This is the number of amperes stored, times the number of hours of life. As an example, a 220 amp-hour battery can store and deliver 22 amps for ten hours, or 2.2 amps for 100 hours, or 220 amps for one hour. These values are under ideal conditions, and should be discounted approximately fifty percent for voltage drop. They are useful, however, as a guide.

The first assumption we make is we will not permit the very high power requirements to draw on the battery bank through the inverter. Specifically, we should not try to run our air conditioners with battery power. If we did, we would soon find our battery bank exhausted, or we would need such a bank of batteries the coach may be too heavy to move. Let us decide, however, that we must power our refrigerator, our cook top, and our water heater with electricity converted to AC through an inverter. These items represent a very high drain on our batteries.

Let us assume the water heater cycle turns on for ten minutes, every two hours, except when some one is using the shower. Each time it cycles, its power consumption is 1500 watts times ten minutes. This is one-sixth of an hour times 1500, and equals 250 watts. Assuming it cycles 15 times a day, it will demand nearly 4000 watts. Divide this by 12 volts and you will need over 300 amp-hours of battery capacity to operate a water heater for one day.

A microwave oven using 750 watts for six minutes (one-tenth of an hour) will consume 75 watts divided by 12 volts which is a little over 6 amp-hours. A 1200 watt toaster on for 3 minutes only uses 5 amp-hours. A 240 watt television on for three hours will use 60 amp-hours. An average residential refrigerator will

use about 200 amp-hours per day. An electrical cook-top used
to prepare meals for about 30 minutes twice a day will use about
200 to 300 amp-hours. Finally, other normal electrical items
such as lighting will use about 50 to 70 amp-hours per day.

Adding up the usage outlined above, we find we need a
battery bank with about 800 amp-hours per day. This size of the
battery bank could be achieved with four 220 amp-hours batteries.
Assuming we have a means of recharging our batteries at the rate
of 200 amperes per hour, it would be necessary to recharge for
four (4) hours per day. (Note: if the batteries were charged at
200 amps, they would probably explode, or melt.) If we wish to
go more than a day without recharging the batteries, we simply
install a larger battery bank, and plan to recharge them for a longer
time.

From the above example, the advantage of propane for
space heating, water heating, refrigeration and cooking is obvious.
Removing these items from our list of power-hungry equipment, a
new assessment reveals an eight-hundred amp-hour battery bank
would allow us to last over a week without recharging our
batteries. However, if we are in a traveling mode, as opposed to
simply being parked, our engine driven alternator could be switched
to charge our house batteries while going down the road to satisfy
even the most severe conditions.

To recap, let us describe a scenario whereby we run our
refrigerator on propane, our water heater on propane, and we
cook and heat with propane. The weather is mild, so air
conditioning is not needed. We have found a delightful spot near
a running stream, and have left our cares at the office. First thing
each morning we make coffee. It takes six minutes to drip through
making three full mugs. We have either toast or frozen waffles
from the toaster taking three minutes. Our day is spent reading,

fishing, hiking, and just sitting, enjoying the peace and beauty of our location. For lunch we heated up some frozen sandwiches in the microwave oven, (this is also a vacation for your bride, remember?). This took six minutes for both sandwiches. Later that evening, we had a frozen desert from the microwave, another six minutes. That night, we enjoyed a movie we brought along in the form of a video tape, for a little over two hours. After her shower, your wife dried her hair with the hair dryer for nine minutes. How many kilowatts did we use, and more important, how many amps did we withdraw from the (battery) bank?

Coffee (1200 watt x .1 hour) .... 120.
Toast or Waffles (1200 watt x 0.05 hours) .... 60.
M/W Sandwiches (720 watt x 0.20 hours) .. 144.
Video Tape Player (120 watt x 2 hours) ...... 240.
Television (180 watt x 2 hours) .... 360.
Hair Dryer (900 watt x 0.15 hours) .... 135.
Utility lighting .... <u>250.</u>
Total watts used = ... **1309.**

With a 12-volt battery bank, you used 1309÷12 =109 amperes, or with a 24-volt battery bank you used about 55 mperes. These figures assume you have an inverter with 100 percent efficiency. In the real world, with losses to heat and other intangibles, you probably used about 120 amps from a 12-volt battery bank. Determine the number of days you would like to repeat this idyllic existence, and size your battery bank accordingly

Power Sources

The most obvious power source is referred to as shore power (to borrow a terms from yachting.) Most modern parks today provide 50 amp hookup, with 30 amp and 15 amp optional. The drawing below show the arrangement for a 50 amp plug.

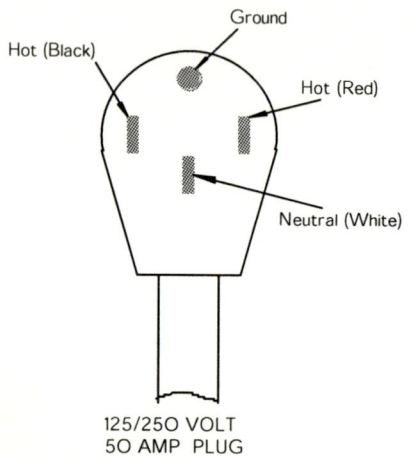

Ground

Hot (Black)

Hot (Red)

Neutral (White)

125/250 VOLT
50 AMP PLUG

Even though the 50 amp plug is appropriate for 240 volts, most parks combine both hot leads to yield 120 volt-50 amp power.

The drawing below is the typical 30 amp plug. This was the standard for all parks for the last 30 years and many parks have not upgraded beyond this service

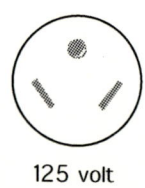

125 volt
30 amp plug

Finally, we have the 15 amp configuration shown to the left.. This is the service you will find in most of the Mexican parks.

125 volt
15 amp plug

OK, now that we have defined our shore power source, we have only one other source of alternating current, which is our generator. (Note: we do not define our inverter and a source for alternating current since it's power source is the battery bank.) Now, it would not do to have both our shore power cord plugged in and our generator running at the same time, so the simplest approach is to have a selector switch which would point to either one, or the other.

A very common piece of equipment, the automatic change-over box, is now available to replace the manual selector switch. This change-over box contains two sets of 50 amp contactors (another term for a heavy duty relay) that will become energized when they feel a current from either the shore power, or the generator, and send power to the distribution panel. Furthermore, this device will create a time delay of approximately 20 seconds to allow the generator to come up to speed and stabilize before delivering the generator power to the panel. Additionally, if the shore power cord is connected, it will disconnect that contactor to favor the generator.

So, we now have a schematic as shown below.

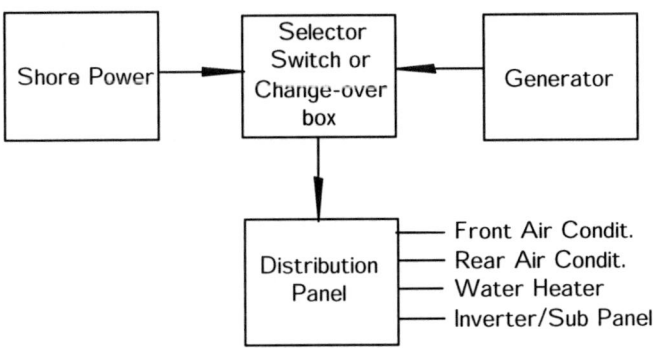

The Schematic shows a few representative circuits leaving the distribution panel. Most notable is the circuit labeled, "Inverter/Sub Panel." This circuit will feed the Inverter, causing it to become a battery charger and continuing on to provide power for the sub panel, which will send power to the lower demand circuits. If no power is felt from either the shore power or the generator, the battery bank will energize the inverter, which will deliver power to the sub panel.

Building on the diagram from the previous page, we add the inverter, sub panel and the battery bank. You will notice the delivery of power between the inverter and the battery bank flows in both directions. If either the shore power or the generator are

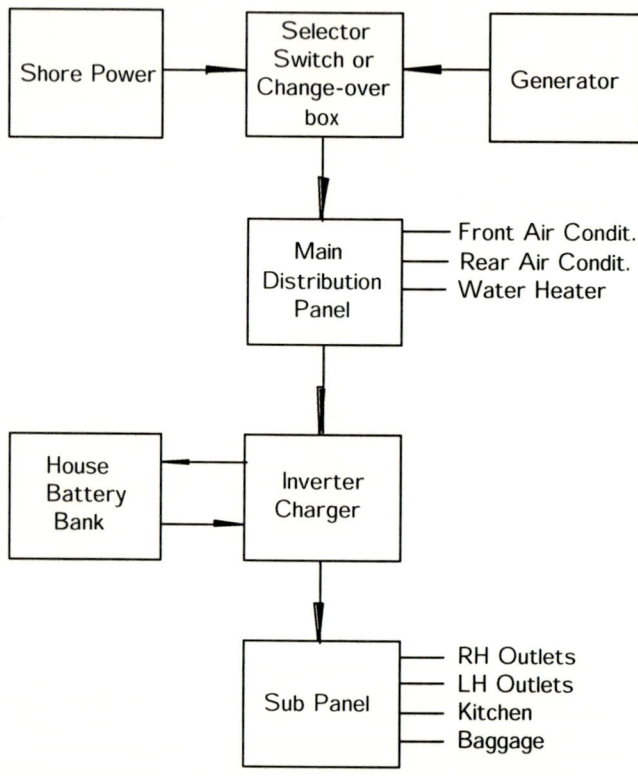

energized, then the inverter is a battery charger and the main panel power flows through the inverter to the sub panel. Otherwise, the battery delivers power to the inverter changing the current into alternating current and sending it to the sub panel. In this case the main panel circuits are inactive.

The diagram below has added another element to the scheme; the direct current, or low voltage circuit breaker panel. This panel is fed from the house battery bank. On the next page the diagram will add the automotive battery bank along with it's charging system and a recommended set of relay switches to permit house battery charging with the alternator while underway and automotive battery charging if parked and plugged into shore power or the generator is running.

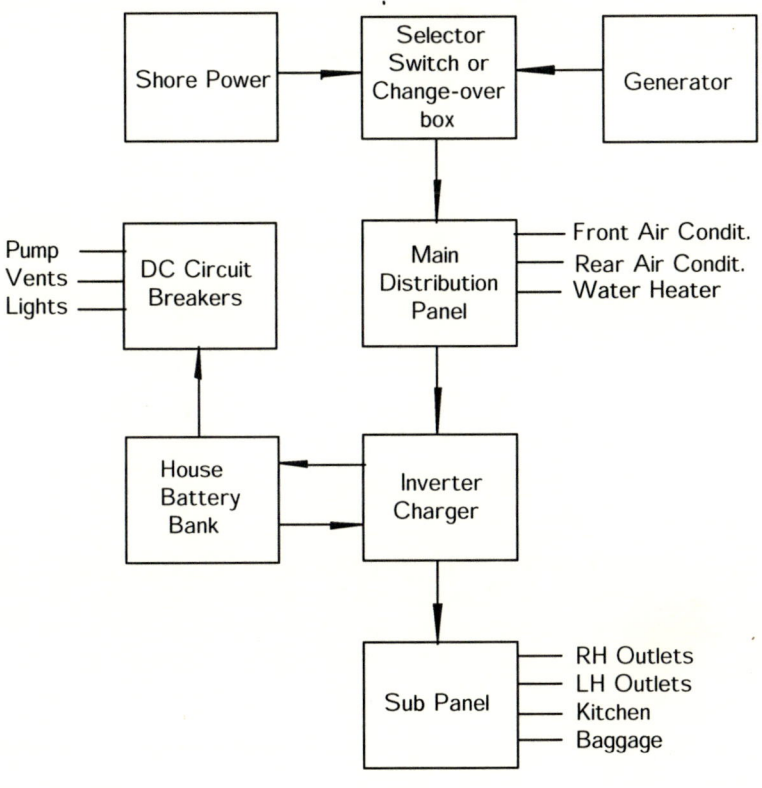

Only a few things could be added to the block diagram shown below; a separate battery for the generator and maybe

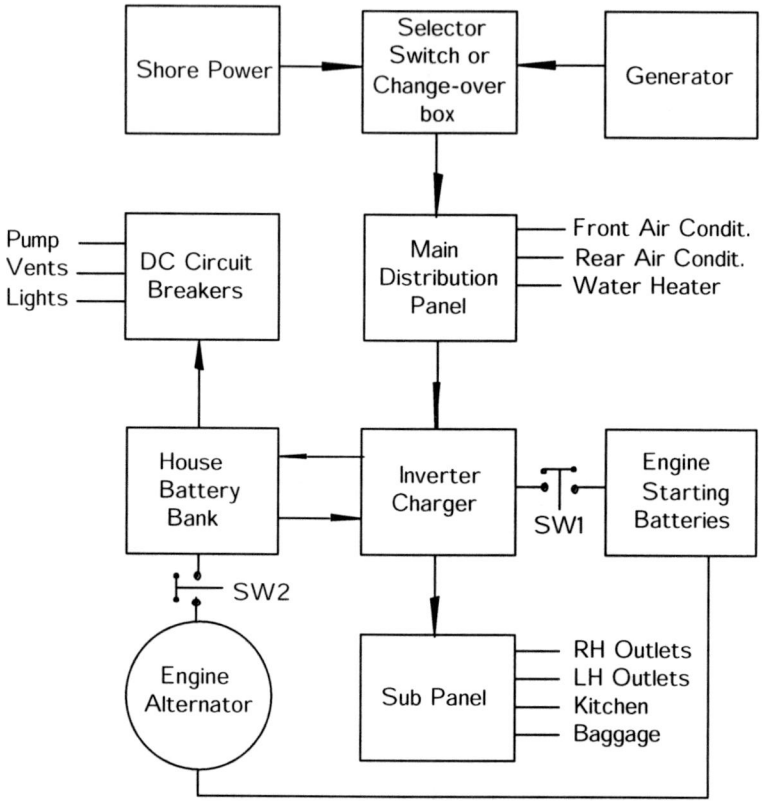

NOTE: SW1 is a 120V relay fed by the main panel to charge
the Engine starting battries when plugged in
SW2 is a 12V relay turned on by the ignitioin switch
to charge the house batteries while underway

solar panels for the house batteries. Otherwise, this scheme is virtually fail-safe. And, we will use this plan for the future discussion in this book.

Circuit Breakers

A variety of circuit breakers are available. Some are made only for alternating current and some are made only for direct current. And, some will work for either. Regardless, all circuit breakers are rated in amps. That is, the number of amperes at which the breaker will disconnect, or trip open.

Most automotive type circuit breakers are designed to automatically reset themselves. These are useful when used in a remote location. The type of breaker we recommend for use in a house panel are the kind which must be manually reset. In fact they work more like a switch, but will disconnect if an power load exceeds their rating. Furthermore, we recommend they type which is appropriate for both alternating and direct current.

Several manufacturers produce this type of breaker. Airpax and Carlingswitch are a couple which come to mind. The drawing shown below is taken from the Carling Technologies catalog. This breaker may be stacked side by side and the mounting panel is easily fabricated, since all one has to do is drill round holes. A 5/8 diameter hole for the toggle switch and 5/32 diameter holes for the mounting screws. A drawing on the next page shows a typical layout of the panel cutout details.

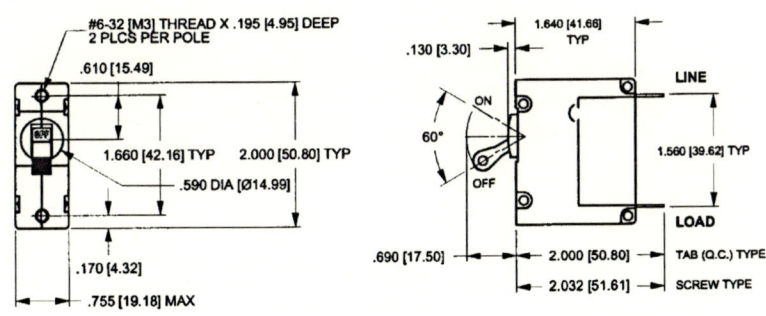

The panel cutout detail shown below is typical for the "A" series toggle handle breaker. The color of the toggle may be selected as white, black, red, or yellow. This might be useful to differentiate bewteen AC main panel, AC sub panel, and DC panel.

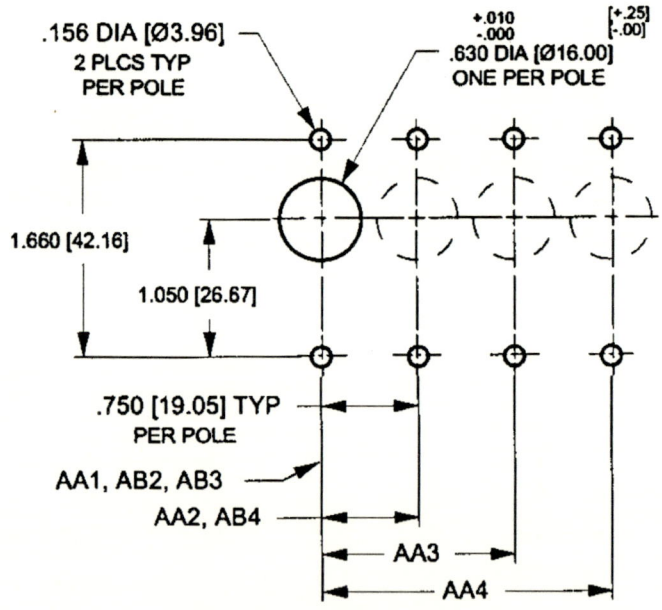

PANEL CUTOUT DETAIL
TOLERANCES ±.005 [±.12]
UNLESS OTHERWISE SPECIFIED

A panel made be configured (a fancy way of saying designed) so that the breakers are all in a single row vertically, or horizontally. Or, it may be designed to have the breakers in multiple rows. Again, either vertically, or horizontally.

It is usually convenient to create two rows in an opposing design. This means when each toggle handle is closest to the center, the circuit is on. When the toggle handle points toward the outside, it is off. This way it is convenient to know the condition of the circuit in the dark.

This picture shows a panel in work. The two rows to the left will be filled with the AC breakers and the two rows in the middle will contain the DC breakers. The two large upper holes on the right will have an AC voltmeter and a DC voltmeter and the lower large holes will be used for the generator gauges, i.e., temperature and oil pressure. The small hole beneath the gauges holes will have the generator start/stop switch. The cutout in the middle of the large holes will contain the water heater ignition switch.

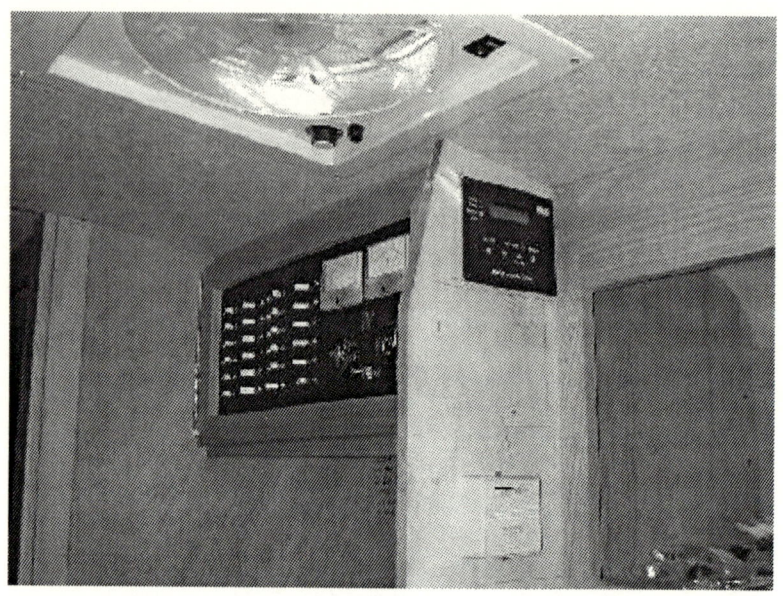

The picture above shows the panel described on the previous page installed. This is a case of mounting the panel over the
refrigerator. It can been seen that the panel is mounted on a frame,
which is installed with a piano hinge. This permits any maintenance or revisions to be done to the back side of the panel.

The inverter remote control panel may also be seen
mounted on a wall perpendicular to the panel. This was done
since there was not enough room on the panel to include this
control. Further down this bulkhead, the furnace thermostat may
be seen.

The drawing on the next page shows a panel design, which
includes both the items on the panel shown above and the inverter
remote control. Furthermore, this panel design is oriented in the
vertical mode. It is designed to be mounted in a frame to be hinged
along one side for maintenance.

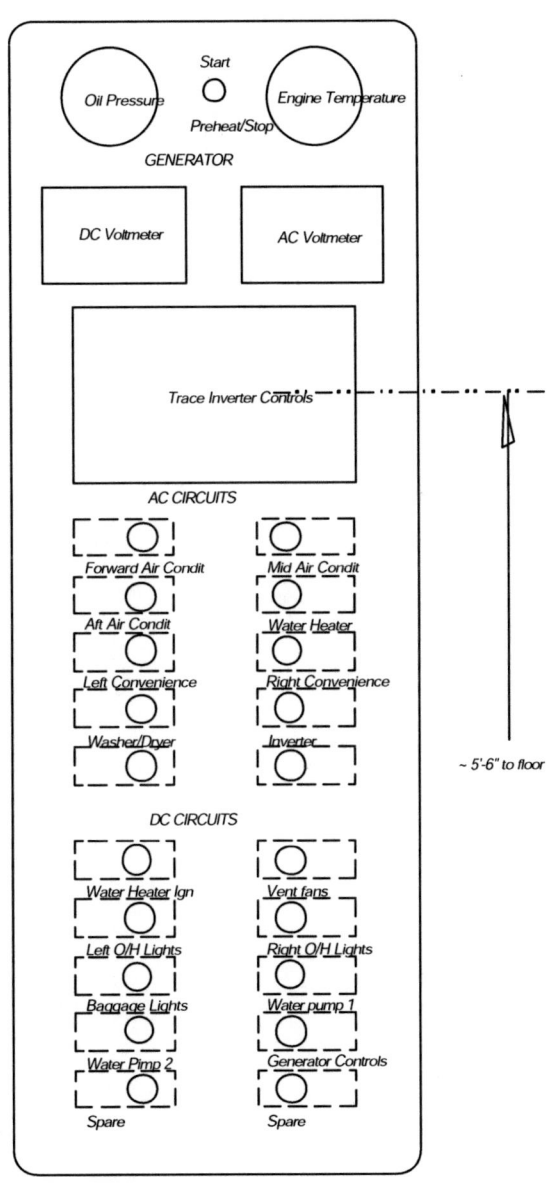

The drawing below shows a representative way of wiring the backside of the fabricated panel. A common bus connects one side of the breakers and is fed from the power source as shown by the notation, "common bus bar (hot)." The lines leading to the notation, "to each individual circuit", are only shown on one side for clarity. Two additional bus bars are installed: one for the

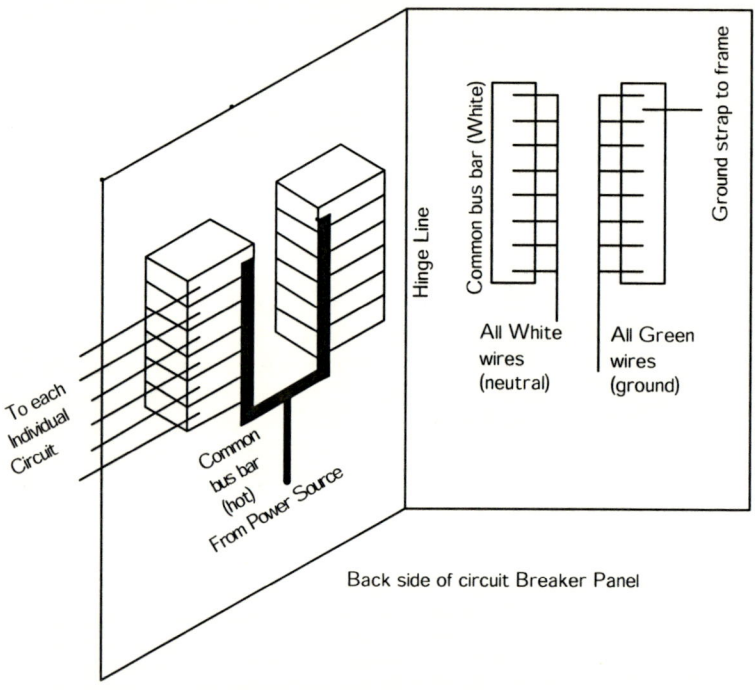

Back side of circuit Breaker Panel

common, or neutral wires, (customarily white wires) and one for the ground wires, customarily green. The bus for the ground wires must be connected to the framework of the coach with a ground strap. The bus bar for the neutral (white) wires may be mounted on a plywood wall, or any convenient dielectric (insulated) surface.

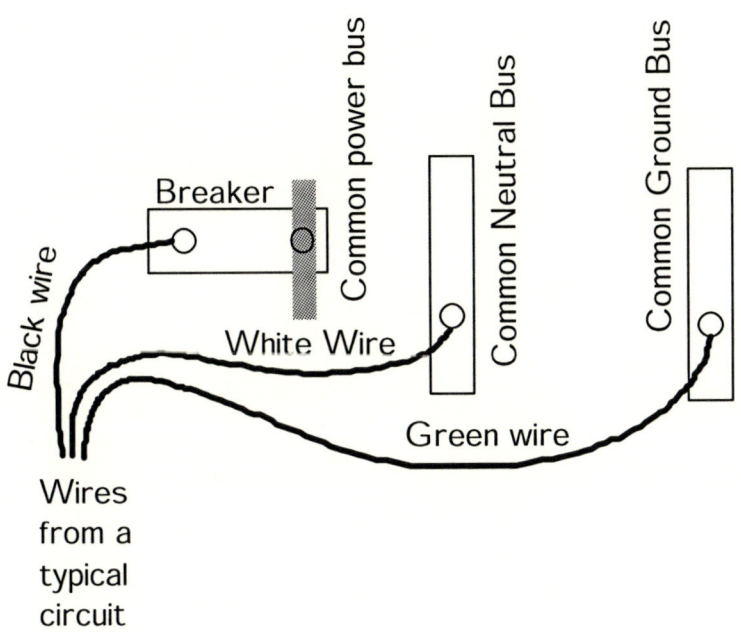

The drawing above shows a typical circuit wiring with the breaker isolated. The color shown is a common convention, but need not be observed. Often the wire labeled, BLACK, may be RED, but for future maintenance, it is important to maintain the convention of the WHITE and GREEN wire colors.

Wiring Diagrams

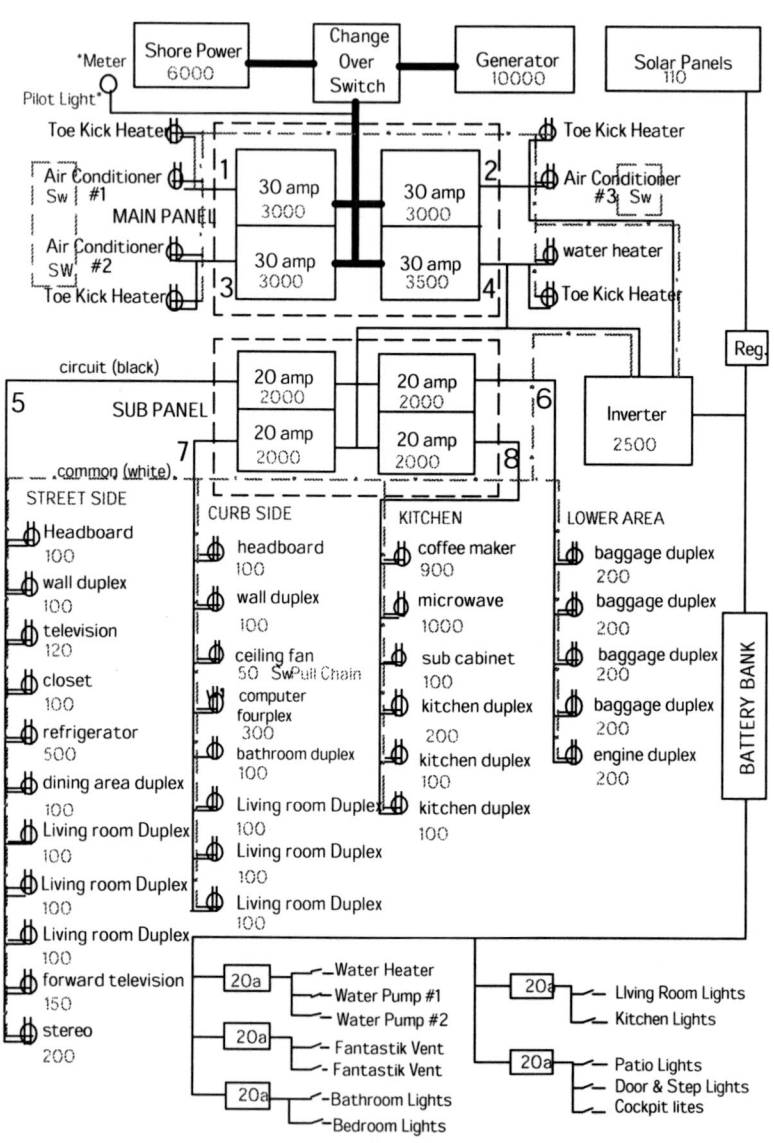

TYPICAL BUS CONVERSION HOUSE CIRCUITRY

The diagram on this page is appropriate only for 24 volt systems such as MCIs and Prevosts

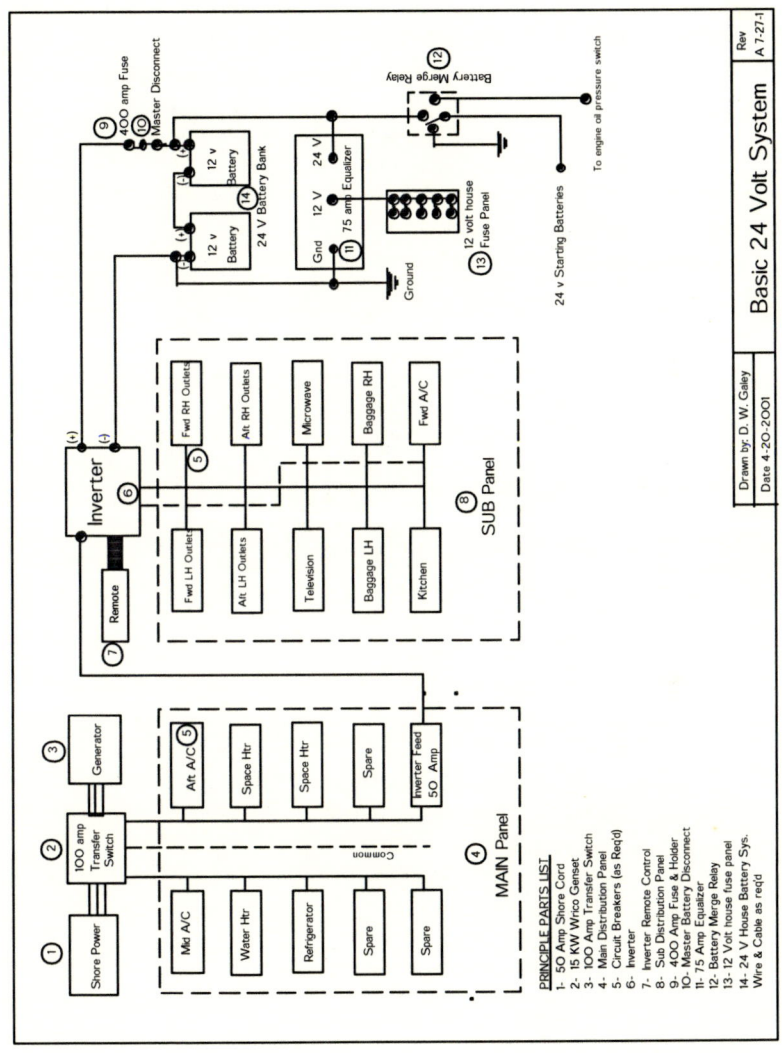

The diagram below shows a multiple station switching circuit. As an example, if you would like to be able to turn on you living room lights from your doorway and turn them off from your kitchen, you might use a three-way switch. However, if you wish to control a light, or other appliance from the doorway, the living room, the kitchen and the bedroom, the circuit shown below will allow you to do that. Many control relays are needed to do this circuit since each of the station switch may be an on/off relay. Marathon and other high line conversion has used this methods of multiple controls.

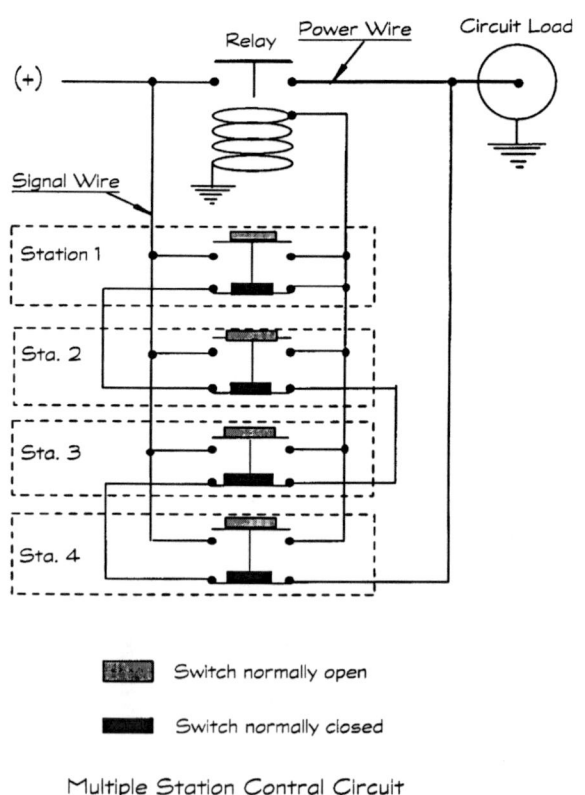

Multiple Station Contral Circuit

For those of you with 24 volt system coaches, it is necessary to create an interface circuit between your coach and a tow vehicle. This is not true of all 24 volt buses since many of them use 12 volt light bulbs. If you need the interface, however, the circuit below will do the job.

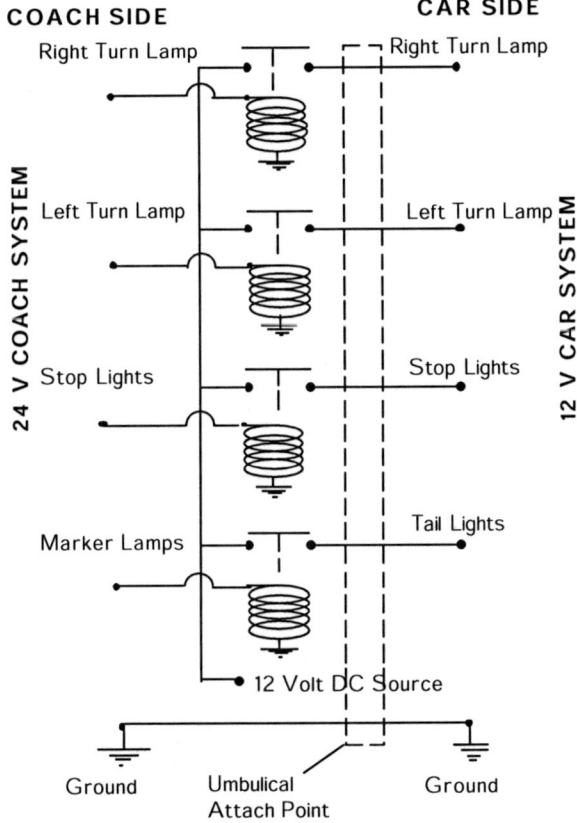

24 V TO 12 V INTERFACE
(for 24 V Coaches)

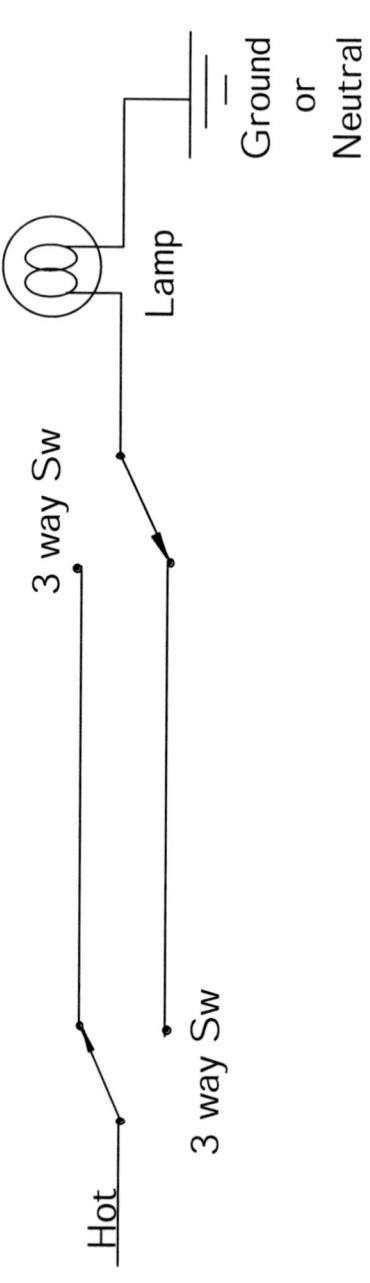

The drawing shown here is a diagram for a three way switching scheme. This allows one to turn on a light, or appliance, from one location and turn it off at another.

You will notice the switches are nothing more than a singe pole, double throw switch. They are quite common and may be purchased at any home supply store or electrical outlet.

Finally, the circuit may be used with an AC circuit or DC circuit. The only difference is the neutral wire must be returned whereas the ground wire can be attached to any convenient body frame.

Tools needed

Several tools are essential for this project. They are:

1. **Crimpers**, such as the style of the Stakon brand. There are other knockoffs, but Stakon is the original. These are used for applying terminals or connectors to the end of wires.

2.. **Wire strippers**. There are a variety of wire strippers, but my favorite are the kind that clamp the wire and remove the insulation in one pliers-like squeeze operation.

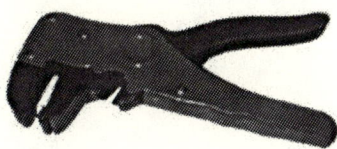

3. A **heat gun** is useful for applying heat shrink tubing.

4. A cheap pair of combination crimpers/strippers/cutters and machine screw cutters to be used only for the machine screw cutter feature. This tool is not suitable for crimping or stripping, but is invaluable for shortening a machine screw. Sometimes, it is necessary to shorten an 8-32 screw from 1 inch to 1/4 inch. This will save many trips to the hardware store.

5. **Hole saws**. These should be one inch, two inch, and three inch in diameter.

6. A **battery operated drill** with a hex head bit holder. A Phillips head screwdriver bit and various size hex head screw sizes.

Supplies

Several items unique to bus wiring will be needed:

1. **Boat cable** is very desirable. It is similar to Romax, i.e., a hot, neutral and ground wire in a single sheath. However, boat cable uses fine stranded wire instead of solid wire as is used in Romax. If you cannot find boat cable, use fine stranded wire instead. The stranded wire sold at Home Depot is coarse, but may be used. Fine stranded wire may normally be purchased at an electronics supply company.

The authors connector assortment showing cable clamps and ties

2. **Crimp style connectors and terminals.** These come in three principal colors for use on various wire sizes. Yellow is used for number 12 and 10 wire. Blue is used on #16 through #14 and Red is for #22 through #18. These terminals are eyelet, male and female spade and fork shapes. The connectors are simply small barrels into which the wires are inserted and crimped.

3. **Shrink tubing** of various sizes to apply after a terminal is attached.

4. **Cable clamps** of various size. These are often plastic loops secured with a single screw. The larger clamps are a metal loop lined with a rubber anti-chafing strip.

6. Nylon plastic **wire ties** of various sizes and colors. Available at Costco or Sam's Club. Also called **Tie Wraps**

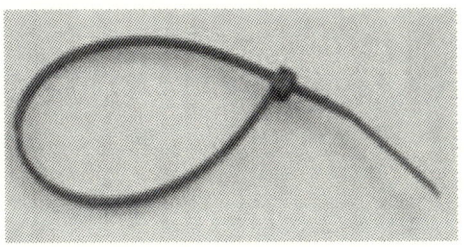

Electrical parts

Duplex Receptacle (commonly called an outlet)

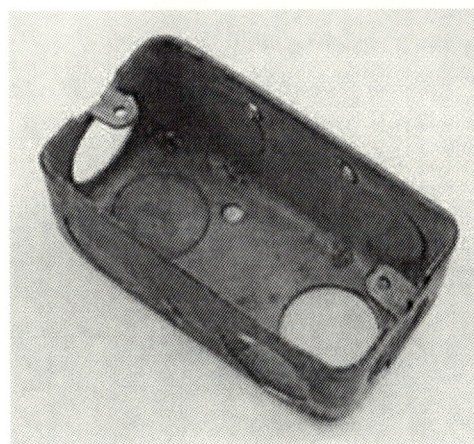

A **Handy box**, in which to mount the receptacle. Most commonly a pressed galvanized steel box with knockouts. Be sure to select those with 1/2 inch knockouts. You may also substitute plastic boxes. My preference is the 1-1/2 x 1-1/2 x 4 box.

Box Clamps: These are used to clamp the wire, romax, or boat cable securely to the box.

Switches: On/Off (single pole single throw)
Three way switch (single pole double throw)
(may also be double pole double throw)

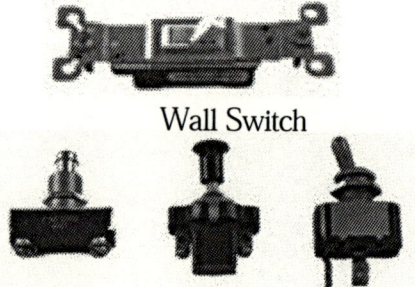

Wall Switch

Momentary   Push/Pull   Toggle

Relays: These are simply switches controlled electrically instead of manually. They may be operated remotely, either manually, or electrically.

Power Relay

Control Relay

Drawing Symbols	
Item	**Symbol**
120 Volt AC Duplex Outlet	
240 Volt AC Receptacle	
12 Volt DC Receptacle	
Relay (electric switch)	
Solenoid valve	
DC Ground	
Switch - single pole single throw (spst)	
Switch - single pole double throw (spdt)	
Switch - double pole double throw (dpdt)	
Switch -spdt - momentary contact	

DAVE GALEY

Now we begin to plan our bus wiring system step by step

Step 1

List all the electrical devices you wish in your conversion

Before a single extension cord can be run, it is important to sit down and list every electrical device you might want in your coach. To help you decide what you may want, I herewith present a shopping list of all the possibilities.

The list is divided into specific areas of interest.

1. Living Area
    - Area Lighting
    - Convenience outlets
        - Table Lamps
    - Television
    - VCR
    - Satellite receiver
    - Mood Lighting
    - Music center
    - Telephone jack
    - GPS
    - Computer
    - Monitor
    - Printer
    - Scanner
    - Speakers
    - Reading lights
    - Air Conditioner
    - Heater
    - Ventilation Fan
    - Monitors
        - Temperature

Video
Systems
TV Antenna controls
2. Dining Area
Toaster
Lighting
Coffee Maker
3 Kitchen Area
Microwave Oven
Cooktop/Oven Igniter
Blender
Instant Hot Water spigot
Convenience Outlet
Ventilation Fan
Coffee Maker
Toaster
Lighting
Refrigerator (AC & DC)

4. Bathroom Area
Lighting
Convenience Outlets
Hair Dryer
Shaver
Electric Toilet
Ventilation Fan

5. Cockpit
Instruments
CB Radio

Stereo/AM/FM/Tape/CD
Rear Vision Monitor
Water Spray Switch
6. Sleeping Area
Casa Blanca Fan
Lighting
Reading Lights
Stereo
Speakers
Mattress Controls
Blanket Power Source
Television & VCR
7. Closets
Lighting
Convenience Outlet
8. Baggage Compartments
Lighting
Convenience Outlets
9. Electrical Control Area
Meter
AC Panel
DC Panel
Generator Controls & gauges
Pump Switch(s)
Water Heater Switch
10. Power Sources
Generator
Inverter
Battery Bank
Master Switch
Fuse
Equalizer

Now that we have a list of possibilities, lets divide the list into separate categories. First, consider all the lighting you may wish. Lighting may be categorized into:

1. Mood, or accent lighting such as, indirect lighting and table lamps.
2. Utility lighting, such as kitchen lights and reading lights.
3. Night lights and security lighting.
4. Patio Lights
5. Docking Lights
6. Spot Lights
7. Assume headlight, marker lights, stop lights and turn signals are O.K.

   If not, plan to re-wire the bus.

   (Shown later in this book)

Step 2

Fill in the tables on the following pages listing those items which will use house current (alternating) and those which will used bus current (direct.)

120 Volt Alternating Current Devices

Item	Watts	Amps	No	Total Watts

12 Volt Direct Current Devices				
Item	Watts	Amps	No	Total Watts

Step 3

Locate and layout all lighting fixture, appliances, and equipment using the block diagrams on the next page. You may refer to a finished drawing as shown on the following page. If necessary make copies of these pages and play with them until you are satisfied with your concept.

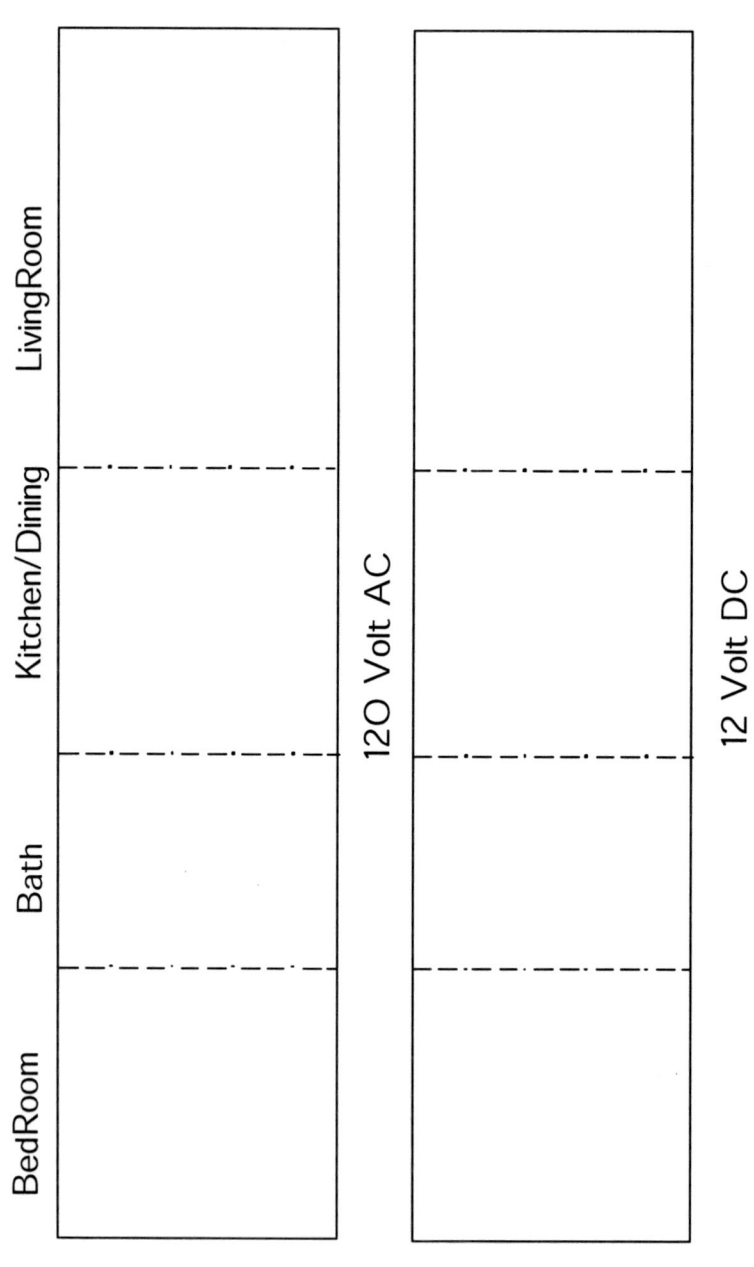

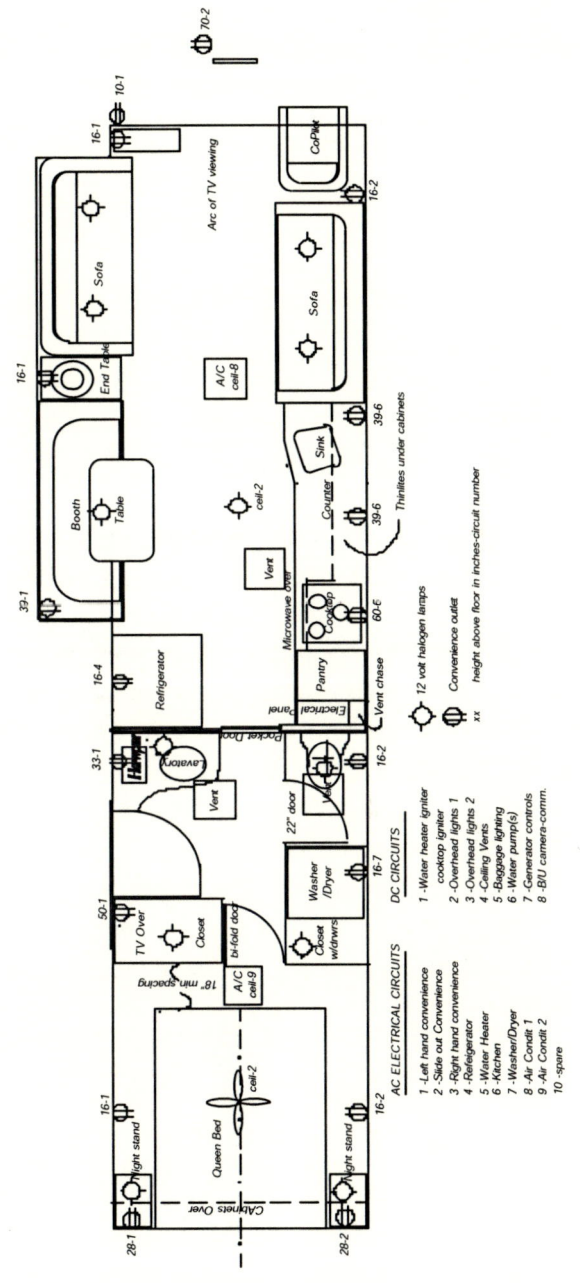

AC ELECTRICAL CIRCUITS

1 -Left hand convenience
2 -Slide out Convenience
3 -Right hand convenience
4 -Refrigerator
5 -Water Heater
6 -Kitchen
7 -Washer/Dryer
8 -Air Condit 1
9 -Air Condit 2
10 -spare

DC CIRCUITS

1 -Water heater igniter
     cooktop igniter
2 -Overhead lights 1
3 -Overhead lights 2
4 -Ceiling Vents
5 -Baggage lighting
6 -Water pump(s)
7 -Generator controls
8 -B/U camera-comm.

○ 12 volt halogen lamps
⊕ Convenience outlet
xx   height above floor in inches-circuit number

Thinilles under cabinets

Step 4

Referring to page 49, create a panel design similar to that drawing, which will meet your requirements. Break up your AC and DC panel and your sub panel using the data learned earlier in this book. At this point, it is important to dedicate a central area, or location for the heart of your system, i.e., your panel and control station. The grid on the next page may be used for sketching your panel layout. Optionally, you may pick up a quadrille pad at any office supply store on which to make your sketches.

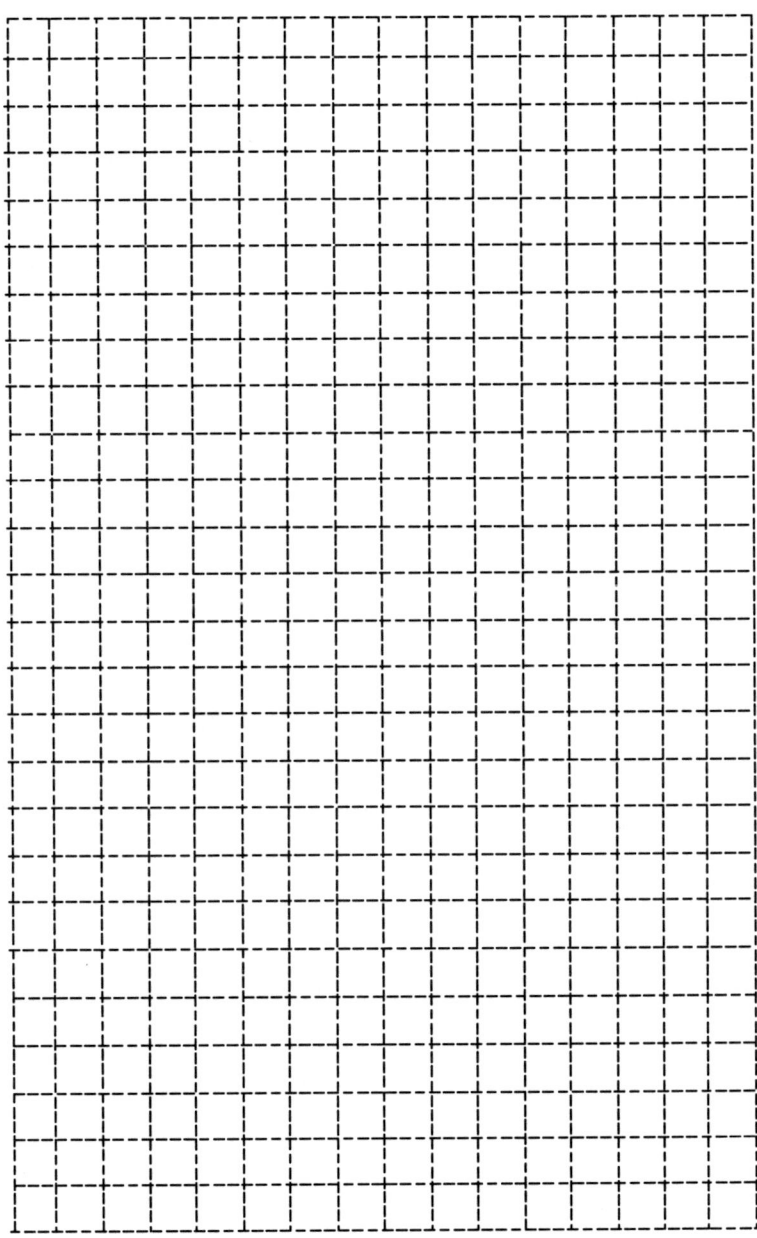

Step 5

Prepare a Parts List or Bill of Materials
Use the table on the next page
(add more times as necessary)

Bill of Materials			
Qty	Item	Unit Cost	Total
	Boxes		
	Duplex Outlets		
	Box Clamps		
	Cable Clamps		
	Eye Terminals		
	Fork Terminals		
	Female Spade		
	Male Spade		
	Wire Ties		
	Wall Switch		
	Toggle Switch		
	Power Relay		
	Control Relay		
	Crimp Connectors		
	Wire Nuts		
	Terminal block		
	# 12 Boat Cable		
	#16 Wire		

Step 6

Locate sources for materials and supplies. This can be a local electrical supply house, Home Depot, Lowes, or even a local hardware store.

For the Generator, Change-over box, and Inverter, I recommend **Wrico International, (541)744-4333, P. O. Box 41555, Eugene, Oregon, 97404-0369.** Contact Dick Wright. Dick has been into bus conversion and converted coach activities for 20 years and is an invaluable source of information.

As to batteries, I have no preference. All batteries are made by a handful of manufacturers who add any marketing companies label to their product, such as DieHard, Trojan, InterState, etc. Basically, there are no differences between lead acid batteries. One form of battery I do recommend is the AGM type battery. This is a lead-acid battery which has **absorbed glass mat** spacers between the plates and they are completely sealed, therefore, no maintenance can be performed on these batteries. I do not recommend the gel-cell battery since it too, is maintenance free, but is very sensitive to over charging.

In the case of the circuit breakers, I recommend a company called **Poco Sales, 8925 Fullbright Ave., Chatsworth, CA 91311, (818)700-8757, www.pocosales.com.** This company stocks AirPax, Carling Switch, etc. The average price of each circuit breaker is just a little over $10 each.

Step 7

Install and secure the generator. The diagram shown below is mostly contained within the generator set wiring. The only requirements are the battery hookup, the connections to the SPDT switch and the leads to the selector switch, or Change-Over-Box. More than one start/stop locations may be employed by simply installing another SPDT momentary switch in parallel with the one shown. The leads from the generator to the Change-Over-Box, or selector switch should be number 6 stranded wire.

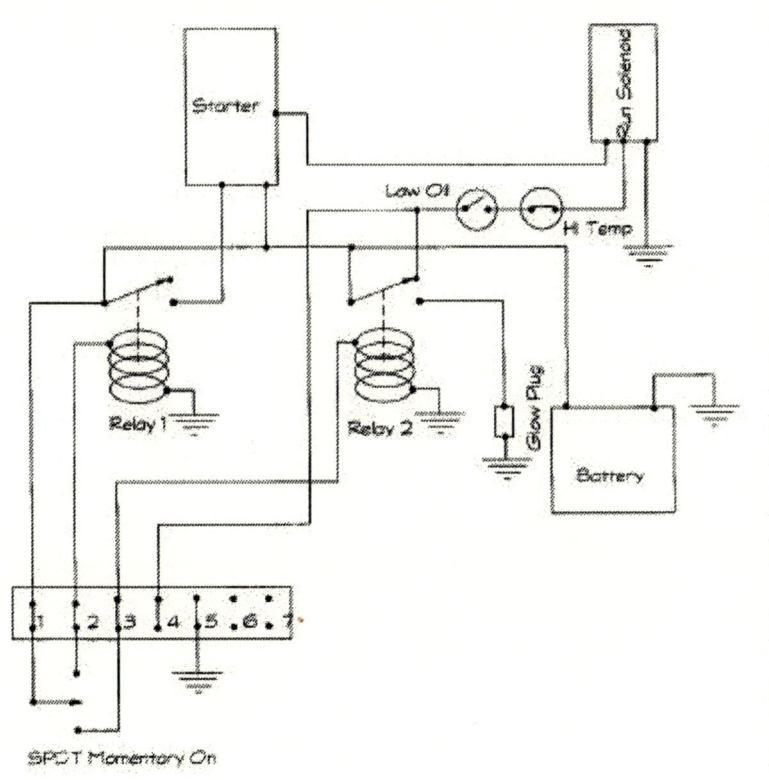

Step 8

Locate and install your inverter. The inverter should be located in a safe and dry spot as near to your battery bank as possible. Ideally, the inverter should be located within five feet of the battery bank. The cable from your battery bank to your inverter should be sized according to the maximum load your inverter can produce. For example, a 3,000 watt inverter can generate nearly 28 AC amps. Therefore, factor this figure times 10 for your battery cables. This means your battery cable must be able to deliver nearly 300 amps, which require at least 4/0 cable. Battery cable is insulated with PVC which is flame-retardant, resistant to fuel, oil, acid, and salt. Welding cable is made with very fine copper wire and insulated with synthetic rubber. It is more flexible than battery cables, especially in cold temperatures. Welding cable is easier to route in tight spaces.

Terminals for your battery cable may be purchased from a welding supply store.

Gage	Standard Insulation	High Temperature Insualtion
14	15 amps	22 amps
12	20 amps	27 amps
10	25 amps	37 amps
8	35 amps	49 amps
6	45 amps	65 amps
4	60 amps	86 amps
2	80 amps	115 amps

Step 9

Install all your rough wiring. This means to locate and attach your boxes, route your boat cable, Romax or stranded wiring from your boxes to your central panel location through your walls, utility chases and ceiling. See the chapter on Wire routing for ideas. Wall outlets are normally 12 to 16 inches above the floor.

After your rough wiring is done, you may install your insulation and close up your walls. After your walls and ceiling are in, you may trim out your electrical sockets.

Keep in mind the convention of attaching the black, or red wire to the bronze colored screw. Attach the white wire to the silver screw and the green wire to the green screw.

Each appliance or item of equipment will have a wiring diagram with it and follow their convention. Use a three light outlet tester to check for correct wiring at all receptacles.

 ' the following faults:

?	Open Grounds
?	Hot-Neutral Reversals
?	Hot-Ground Reversals
?	Open Neutrals
?	Open Hots

And they generally cost less than $10

Step 10

Finally, plug into shore power and test all your circuits and appliances. See that your inverter is charging your batteries. Troubleshoot any problems that show up. Then light off your generator and do the same thing.

Now, disconnect from shore power and shut down your generator and test all the circuits and appliances fed by your inverter. Program you inverter according to the instruction manual. Troubleshoot any problems.

Bus Automotive Circuitry

The chapter to follow is a set of instructions to build a replacement panel for the automotive section of the bus. That is, it is the control panel containing the breakers and relays controlling the action of the headlights, the marker lights, the turn signals, the horn and the stop (brake) lights.

This chapter replaces and earlier discontinued publication title, "Replacement Electrical Control Panel."

Introduction

Many of the older buses the self conversion specialist choose to transform into a luxury motorhome have suspect wiring. After 25, 30 and even 40 years of wear and tear, vibration and chafing, wiring in a vehicle can become tired and unreliable. Unlike residential or commercial wiring, the installation in a moving vehicle may, after time, become erratic, behaving properly sometimes and not others. One typical example of this behavior is headlights. I have experienced cases where headlights would extinguish altogether when the dimmer switch was depressed. This can become quite upsetting when trying to negotiate a mountain curve after being flashed by an oncoming, thoughtless road warrior.

The object of this presentation is to provide the scheme to replace this antique wiring with modern relays, new wiring and automatic re-settable breakers. Generally, your old switches should be fine, but this is a choice of the owner. However, switches are one item which are constantly being cycled, so they have a tendency to fail after time. If you have any suspicions, the switches should be replaced. It is a good idea to replace all the light bulbs when going thought this process. This way you will be assured of a fresh system.

Instructions

The diagram given is a modification of a factory design with the items necessary to satisfy the DOT, removed. That is, such amenities used for passenger safety and comfort which do not pertain to the needs of a motorhome have been eliminated.

One note about relays: The relay specified may be substituted. A common substitution is a relay with 5 terminals instead of four. The fifth terminal is simply not used. A five terminal relay is a universal type in that it can be used to make a contact or break a contact. This means it has the option to be used as *normally open*, or *normally closed*. If your supplier can only furnish you with the universal relay, simply ignore the center terminal, using the outer four terminals.

It will be necessary to fabricate a mounting plate. This is customarily a piece of aluminum sheet metal approximately one-sixteenth inch thick and about 16" x 20" rectangular. These dimensions are not critical. They should be chosen to accommodate mounting the elements, i.e.., relays, terminals and breakers, and to be easily mounted at some convenient location in the bus. That location should be near the drivers position, but not mandatory.

One other component which must be fabricated is a battery terminal block. This may be made from any dielectric, such as micarta, hardwood, plastic or corian. All that is important is to have a screw thread to which the battery cable may be attached and feeding the various circuit breakers and terminal on the assembly. And, this battery terminal block must be electrically isolated from the mounting panel.

The components should be mounted on the panel in any convenient pattern. The mounting diagram is a suggestion only. It may be used as a guide but if another pattern make more sense to your application, use it.

All the wires are numbered and it is only necessary to connect them by the number. All the circuit breakers are lettered alphabetically, omitting only the letter I and O.

The configuration of the breakers may be either the spade type terminal or the screw type terminal. They may have their own mounting lugs or you may have to purchase a mounting receptacle. The terminal strips may be the spade lug type or the screw terminal type. These features are not important. The importance is mainly what is available at your local auto supply store. Every items in the parts list is commonly available at any auto parts supply store with the exception of the battery terminal and the mounting plate.

I recommend a good quality wire terminal crimper tool. The best one made is by Stak-On but this tool is now quite expensive. Be sure to test all your terminal fitting by tugging on them to be sure they are properly attached.

After your assembly is completed, bench test it to satisfy it does what you expected. A simple test device may consist of a 12 volt lamp with some alligator clips. Use a spare battery to apply 12 VDC to the battery post and use a jumper wire with alligator clips to simulate a switch closing. Then go through each system actuating each relay to prove it's function and that it is working properly. After the bench test is completed, you are ready to install into your coach.

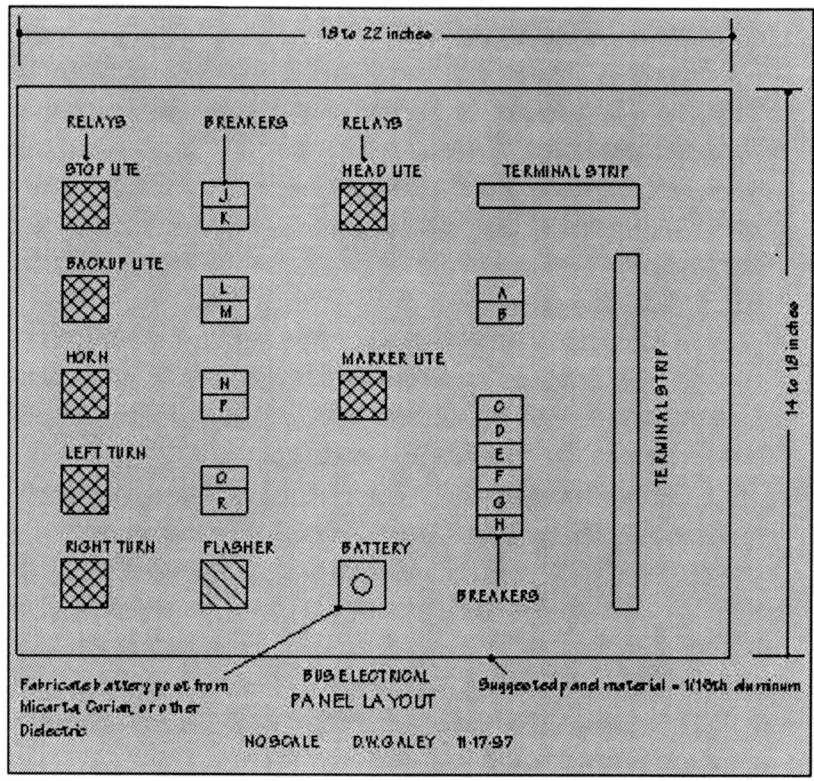

86

This photograph shows a typical arrangement of the panel design shown at the left.

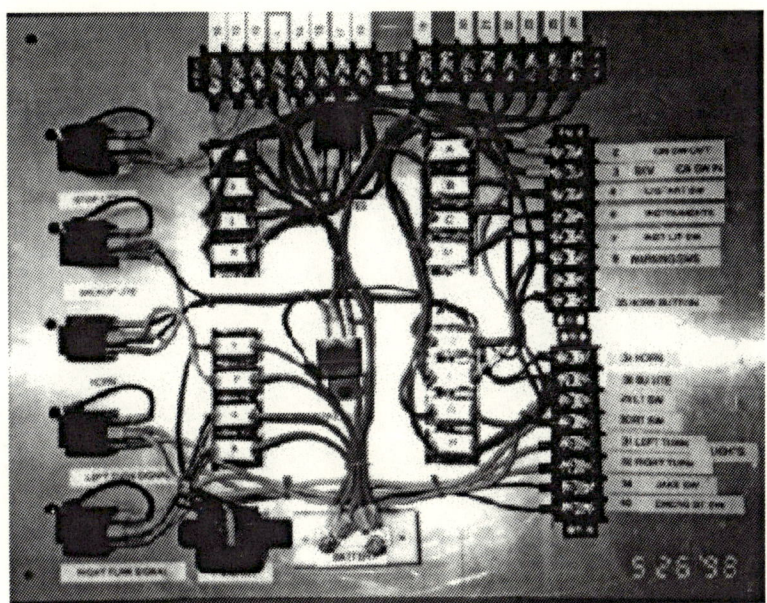

Another picture of a panel design

This picture show a panel installed in the lower door of an Eagle coach underneath the drivers position

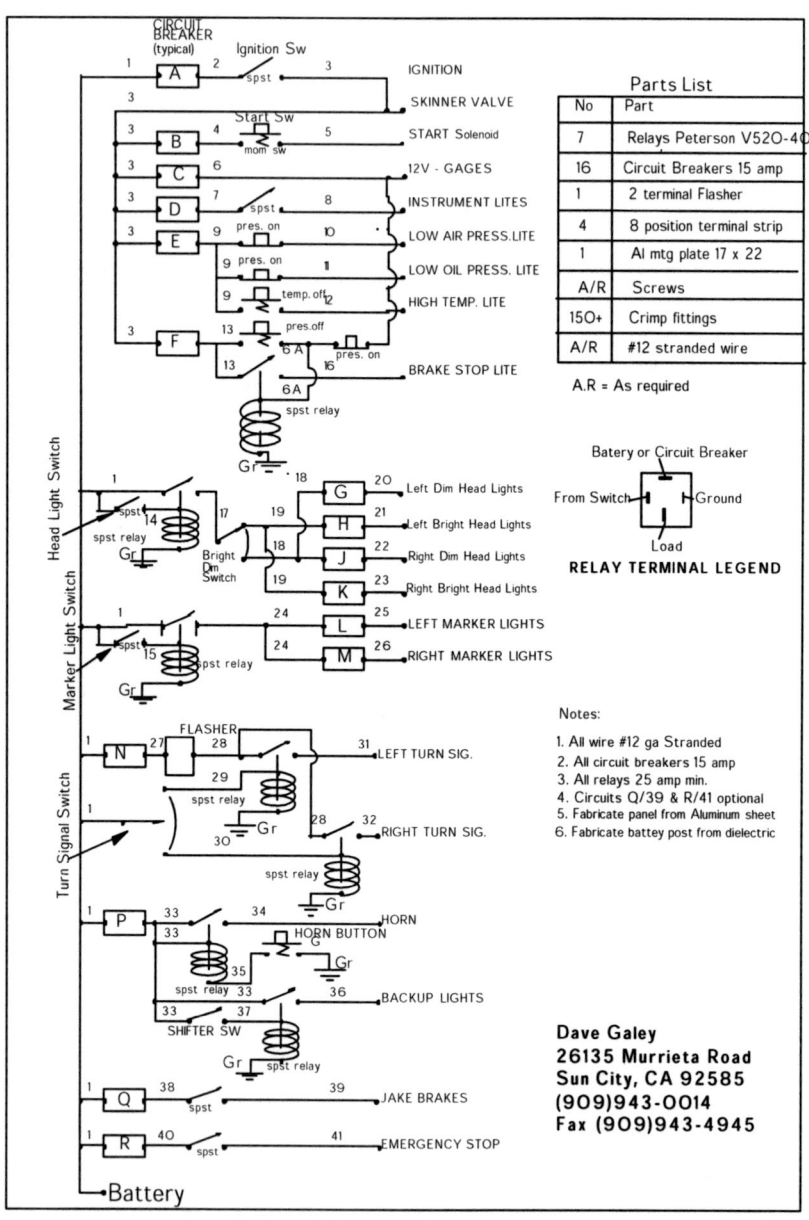

Parts List

No	Part
7	Relays Peterson V520-40
16	Circuit Breakers 15 amp
1	2 terminal Flasher
4	8 position terminal strip
1	Al mtg plate 17 x 22
A/R	Screws
150+	Crimp fittings
A/R	#12 stranded wire

A.R = As required

RELAY TERMINAL LEGEND

Notes:

1. All wire #12 ga Stranded
2. All circuit breakers 15 amp
3. All relays 25 amp min.
4. Circuits Q/39 & R/41 optional
5. Fabricate panel from Aluminum sheet
6. Fabricate battey post from dielectric

Dave Galey
26135 Murrieta Road
Sun City, CA 92585
(909)943-0014
Fax (909)943-4945

Electrical Panel Installation Instructions

1. Connect the Battery to either of the BATTERY posts (suggest you do this last).

2. Connect terminal 2 to the ignition on/off switch.

3. Connect terminal 3 to the other side of the ignition on/off switch. Also connect this side to the Skinner valve.

4. Connect terminal 4 to the momentary start switch. Connect the other side of this switch to the start solenoid.

5. Connect terminal 6 to the instruments (gauges). Also connect to normally closed pressure switch for the brake system.

6. Connect Terminal 7 to the instrument light on/off switch. Connect other side to instrument lights.

7. Connect terminal 9 to the normally closed low air light switch, the normally closed low oil light switch, and the normally open high temperature light switch.

8. Connect terminal 13 to the normally open air pressure switch of the brake system.

9. Connect terminal 6a to the other side of the normally closed air pressure switch of the brake system.

10. Connect terminal 16 to the brake lights.

11. Connect terminal 1 to one side of the headlight on/off switch, to one side of the marker light on/off switch and to the center terminal of the turn signal switch.

12. Connect terminal 1A to the other side of the headlight on/off switch.

13. Connect terminal 1B to the other side of the marker lights on/off switch.

14. Connect terminal 17 to the common position of the Bright/Dimmer selection switch.

15. Connect terminal 18 to the Dimmer light position of the Bright/Dimmer selection switch.

16. Connect terminal 19 to the Bright light position of the Bright/Dimmer selection switch.

17. Connect terminal 20 to the Left headlight dim position

18. Connect terminal 21 to the Left headlight bright position.

19. Connect terminal 22 to the Right headlight dim position.

20. Connect terminal 23 to the Right headlight bright position.

21. Connect terminal 25 to the left set of marker lights.

22. Connect terminal 26 to the right set of marker lights.

23. Connect terminal 31 to the left turn signal lights

24. Connect terminal 32 to the right turn signal lights.

25. Connect terminal 29 to the left turn position of the turn signal switch.

26. Connect terminal 30 to the right turn position of the turn signal switch.

27. Connect terminal 35 to one side of the horn button. Ground the other side of this switch.

28. Connect terminal 34 to the horn.

29. Connect terminal 38 to the Jake Brake switch. Connect the other side to the Jake Brakes.

30. Connect terminal 40 to the emergency shut down switch. Connect the other side to the emergency shut down solenoid.

Ampere Draw - Wattage per Voltage				
Wattage	12V	24V	120V	240V
100	8.4	4.2	.84	.42
200	16.7	8.4	1.7	.84
300	25.0	12.5	2.5	1.3
400	34.0	16.7	3.4	1.7
500	41.7	21.0	4.2	2.1
1000	84.0	42.0	8.4	4.2
1500	125.0	63.0	12.5	6.3
2000	167.0	84.0	16.7	8.4
2500	209.0	105.0	21.0	10.5

Conclusions

This book should provide the basic information for an average guy to do his own wiring. If there is any questions, contact an electrician, or you may give me a call at (909)943-0014.

One point I would like to emphasis is the maintenance of your equipment. One example of a NoNo is the use of damaged adapters. I have seen a case where a ground prong from an adapter had been removed so as to defeat a ground-fault-interrupter outlet. If this adapter is used, and the power source is inserted in a reversed mode, the frame of the coach become electrified (HOT), and anyone leaning against the bus with bare feet will have a shocking experience.

Be careful with electricity. You have the advantage of being able to test your installation any time you wish by simple plugging in your shore cord. Remember when it is plugged in, and do not work on the system when it is.

Any suggestion to improve this presentation will be gratefully appreciated and you may send your suggestion to:

Winlock Publishing
26135 Murrieta Road
Sun City, CA 92585

Index

Symbols

A

B

C

Poco Sales 78
Power Distribution 17
Power Sources 40
propane 29

R

residential service 28

S

short circui 15
solar panels 35
solid state inverter 33
Start-up load 28
sub panel 21
Supplies 59

T

three way switch 56
Tools needed 57

V

voltage 17

W

wall plug 15
wattage 17
Wind generators 36
wire chase 26
Wire Routing 25
Wiring Diagrams 52
Wrico International 78

The Motor Coaching Bible

This is a complete handbook for all those with a motorhome, planning to purchase a motorhome or planning to upgrade. Seven guest authors have contributed chapters covering insurance, associations, published material and technical data.

Useful check lists are included along with instructions for towing and camping locations and governments parks. A ten page index is included for fast reference to subjects.

ISBN 1-890461-14-8
Price: US$24.95
408 pages
Illustrated
Paper Perfect Bound

The Joys of Busing

Fifteen Years of screw-ups confessed by the author. Although,it was intended to be humor, by accident, this books has become a reverse maintenance manual.

It is an education in on-the-road repairs. Laugh at the mishaps of the author, and others, and experience the breakdowns without the anguish.

A collection of hilarious adventures while motoring around the North American continent in a converted bus.

ISBN 0-9649437-2-7
Price: US$19.95
220 pages
Illustrated
Paper Perfect Bound

Classy Cabinets for Converted Coaches

This book is written for the accountant, UPS driver, or salesman. The professional cabinetmenker already knows everything in this book.

It gives tricks to make templates to match contours and techniques for steam bending. Attachment methods are shown and strength tables are included

ISBN 1-890461-03-2
Price: US$19.95
152 pages
Illustrated
Comb Bound

Fascinating Fastener Facts

Included are strength table for nuts, bolts, screws, glues, welds, adhesives and rivets. An occasional opinion by the author spices up anotherwise, dull subject. A special section titled, *Things to Cry Over* will outline fastener problems and solutions.

ISBN 1-890461-00-8
Price: US$14.95
128 pages
Illustrated
Paper Perfect Bound

The Gospel of Gauges

This book contains a list of all the gauges, instruments, and monitors a person might considers installing in their bus conversion.It explains what a guage will depicts and how to install and wire, or plumb the gauge

ISBN 1-890461-01-6
Price US$9.95
80 Pages
Illustrated
Comb bound

Slide Out Rooms Mechanics amd Structures

This book explores the various options for creating an expanding room in a recreational vehicle. It is fairly heavy on structural theory but also includes actuation methods, alignment solutions, seals, latching and and a proposed electrical diagram.

ISBN 1-890461-11.3
Price US$19.95
92 Pages
Illustrated

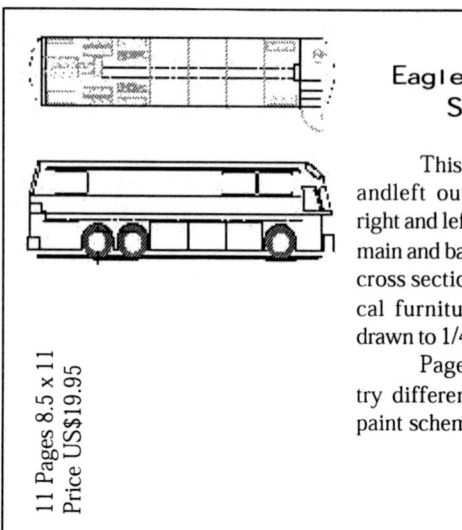

Eagle Planning Sheets

This kit includes (1) right andleft outboard profiles, (2) right and left inboard profiles, (3) main and baggage floor plans, (4) cross sections, and a set of typical furniture and apppliances drawn to 1/4 inch to the foot scale

Pages may be copied to try different arrangements and paint schemes

11 Pages 8.5 x 11
Price US$19.95

Busin' Bits

A Collection of Articles pertaining to the conversion of a crummy old tour bus into a luxurious motorhome. Nearly 40 articles on too many subjects to name. Buy this and pitch your old magazines.

ISBN: 1-890461-23-7   Price $19.95
164 pages   Ilustrated   Perfect Bound

The Bus Converter's Bible

This book is divided into Six Sections:

1 - Structural Modifications
2 - Plumbing
3 - Electrical Systems
4 - Heating and Air Conditioning
5 - Interior Design
6 - Exterior Design
    Designed to guide the novice or professional through the complexities of Luxury Motor coach construction. Especially useful for those planning to buy a converted coach or have one converted for them.

ISBN 0-9649437-4-3
Price: US$49.95
280 pages
Illustrated
Paper Perfect Bound

Black & Blue Highways

    This is the story of a do-it-yourself bus driver and his wife zigzagging across the US and Canada in a home made bus conversion. Only three breakddowns occurred and were repaired with the help of professionals and good samaritans.
    They traveld over 10,000 miles and had only $1,000 in repair bills . . . not bad!
    As he is an Elk, they stayed in over 25 Elk's Lodges enroute.

ISBN 1-891461-22-9
Price U$14.95
112 Pages
Paper Perfect Bound

Name _____

Address _____

City _____

State _____

Zip _____

Phone _____

The Bus Converter's Bible	$49.95
The Motor coaching Bible	$24.95
The Joys of busing	$19.95
The Gospel of Gauges	$9.95
Classy Cabinets	$19.95
Slide Out Rooms	$19.95
Fascinating Fasteners	$14.95
Busin' Bits	$19.95
Eagle Planning sheets	$19.95
Black & Blue highways	$14.95
Bus Wiring for Bus nuts	$29.95

Send to: Winlock Galey
        26135 Murrieta Road
        Sun City, CA 92585

or Call: (909)943-0014 or Fax (909)943-4945

Visa ____ MasterCard _____ Amex ____ Discover ____

Card Number _____

Expiration _____ Signed _____

WG

WG

WG

Printed in the United States
85322LV00002B/49-54/A